Music in the early years

D0877546

Research findings repeatedly show that music is one of the subjects which teachers feel least confident to tackle. There are many reasons for this, not least being the lack of appropriate guidance and training. This book is designed to help overcome these problems by providing class teachers with clear advice on how to plan, resource and deliver a comprehensive programme which will challenge their pupils and enable them to progress and meet national requirements. The book includes examples and activities which can be used as a basis for in-service training within schools, particularly for teachers who regard themselves as non-specialists.

Aelwyn Pugh is an LEA Inspector for Curriculum with Music. **Lesley Pugh** is a freelance music teacher of nursery, infant and junior pupils.

Teaching and learning in the first three years of school
Series Editor *Joy Palmer*

This innovative and up-to-date series is concerned specifically with curriculum practice in the first three years of school. Each book includes guidance on:

- subject content
- planning and organisation
- assessment and record-keeping
- in-service training

This practical advice is placed in the context of the National Curriculum and the latest theoretical work on how children learn at this age and what experiences they bring to their early years in the classroom.

Other books in the series:

Geography in the Early Years
Joy Palmer

History in the Early Years
Hilary Cooper

Mathematics in the Early Years
Wendy Clemson and David Clemson

Physical Education in the Early Years
Pauline Wetton

Music in the early years

Aelwyn and Lesley Pugh

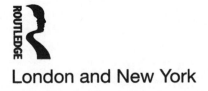

London and New York

First published 1998
by Routledge
11 New Fetter Lane, London EC4P 4EE

Simultaneously published in the USA and Canada
by Routledge
29 West 35th Street, New York, NY 10001

Typeset in Palatino by M Rules
Printed and bound in Great Britain by
Page Brothers (Norwich) Ltd

British Library Cataloguing in Publication Data
A catalogue record for this book is available from the British
Library

Library of Congress Cataloging in Publication Data
Pugh, Aelwyn.
  Music in the early years / Aelwyn and Lesley Pugh.
  p. cm. – (Teaching and learning in the first three of
  school)
  Includes bibliographical references.
  1. School music – Instruction and study. I. Pugh, Lesley.
  II. Series.
  MT1.P847 1998
  372.87–dc21
  97-45590
  CIP
  MN

ISBN 0–415–14181–8

TO OUR DAUGHTER RHIANNON
AND
OUR GODSON EDWARD

Contents

Figures

Tables

Series editor's preface

Each book in this series focuses on a specific curriculum area. The series relates relevant learning theory or a rationale for early years learning to the practical development and implementation of subject-based topics and classroom activities at the infant level (i.e., Reception, Year 1, Year 2). It seems that the majority of existing books on primary education and the primary curriculum focus on pupils aged 7–11 years. It is hoped that this series presents a refreshing and much needed change in that it specifically addresses the first three years in school.

Each volume is intended to be an up-to-date, judicious mix of theory and practical classroom application, offering a wealth of background information, ideas and advice to all concerned with planning, implementing, monitoring and evaluating teaching and learning in the first three years in school. Theoretical perspectives are presented in a lively and interesting way, drawing upon recent classroom research findings wherever possible. Case studies and activities from a range of classrooms and schools illuminate many of the substantial issues related to the subject area in question.

Readers will find a similar pattern of contents in all the books in the series. Each discusses the early learning environment, transition from home- to school-based learning, and addresses the key questions of what this means for the early years teacher and the curriculum. Such discussion inevitably incorporates ideas on the knowledge which young children may have of subjects and an overview of the subject matter itself which is under scrutiny. As the thrust of the series is towards young children learning subjects, albeit in a holistic way, no doubt readers will wish to consider what is an appropriate content or rationale for the subject in the early years. Having considered young children as learners, what they are bringing into school in terms of prior knowledge, the teacher's task and the subject matter itself, each book then turns its attention to appropriate methods of planning, organising, implementing and evaluating teaching and learning activities. Crucial matters such as assessment, evaluation and record-keeping are dealt with in their own right, and are also referred to and discussed in ongoing examples of good practice. Each book concludes with useful suggestions for further staffroom discussion/INSET activities and advice on resources.

As a whole, the series aims to be inspirational and forward-looking. As all readers know so well, the National Curriculum is not 'written in concrete'. Education is a dynamic process. While taking due account of the essential National Curriculum framework, authors go far beyond the level of description of rigid content guidelines to highlight *principles* for teaching and learning. Furthermore, they incorporate two key messages which surely underpin successful, reflective education, namely 'vision' and 'enthusiasm'. It is hoped that students and teachers will be inspired and assisted in their task of implementing successful and progressive plans which help young learners to make sense of their world and the key areas of knowledge within it.

Joy A. Palmer

Foreword

An ancestor only ever learnt to speak one sentence of English. 'I can't', she would say, 'is a sluggard too lazy to work'. It probably was and still is a very apposite statement in a wide range of circumstances. However, one context in which it very rarely applies is when teachers say: 'I can't sing'; 'I can't compose'; 'I can't play an instrument'. These people's claims stem not from laziness but from a whole welter of factors: being told by their teachers that they were 'tone deaf', being dismissed from the school percussion band for being 'unmusical', being told to mime in hymn practices; damage which has been further reinforced by inadequate help during their teacher training and at later points in their career.

In the past, such a situation was tolerated because there was no requirement for schools to teach music. Therefore, if staff felt that they could not teach it and no alternative provision could be found, the subject was simply ignored. Since the advent of the National Curriculum, however, and the legal requirement for all pupils aged between 5 and 14 to be taught music, the situation is having to be addressed.

This book is intended to help in that process. It is designed for generalist class teachers, to help them clarify their thoughts about music and to find a way through what can seem a rather daunting subject. It is also designed for coordinators who, in every subject, assume an increasingly important role in helping their colleagues extend their knowledge, skills and understanding. The third audience at whom it is directed are teachers in training and those who supervise their work, whether within school or in higher education institutions.

The book falls into four broad sections. Chapters 1 to 3 focus on why we should teach music, what the focus of work in this area should be and what we should know of young children's development prior to their embarking on formal schooling. Chapters 4 to 10 concentrate on how music might be delivered, while Chapters 11 to 15 discuss issues of planning, monitoring and resourcing. The final section consists of a series of activities which could be used as the basis of school-based in-service training. Some readers might find aspects of this last section too detailed or over-prescriptive but, as explained in Chapter 16, we feel that there are strong reasons to support such an approach.

In keeping with other books in this series, we have related theory to practice and have tried to illustrate our arguments with illustrations drawn from infant classrooms in which we have taught, or acted as observers, in several parts of the country. We can say with confidence, therefore, that the ideas presented here work and are applicable to a variety of circumstances. They are neither exhaustive nor definitive, but are presented as a spring board to enable teachers to give their pupils musical experiences that are worthwhile and valuable.

Acknowledgements

Our thanks are due to colleagues, students and pupils past and present who have helped us develop our thinking.

Special thanks are due to Malik Killen for his kind help in preparing the typescript.

Chapter 1

Why should we teach music?

THE CURRENT STATUS OF MUSIC EDUCATION

The establishment of the National Curriculum in the early 1990s was a major milestone in the history of music education in this country. For the first time since the passing of the 1870 Education Act, it became a legal requirement that all pupils aged 5–14 should be taught music. More recently, music has also had to be included in any recognised nursery provision under the general heading of Creative Development. In 1993, with the establishment of the Office for Standards in Education (OFSTED), a regular cycle of inspections was introduced to ensure that these and other statutory requirements were met in all state schools. On the surface, therefore, all seems to be well.

THREATS TO THE CURRENT SITUATION

However, the picture is not that simple. Enshrining the requirement to teach a subject in law may be helpful but legislation can be changed to match political whims, fashions and expediency. The events leading to the creation of the National Curriculum showed this only too clearly, especially where music was concerned. At the outset, music was to be taught to all pupils up to the age of 16, and pupils were to be tested in it at the end of each key stage. Through successive stages of drafting and consultation, however, its position was eroded until eventually it became a requirement only for Key Stages 1–3 and pupils no longer had to be tested formally in it.

Although the National Curriculum established a requirement for all pupils to be taught a broad, balanced curriculum, there has been a gradual erosion of that principle. The thrust towards improving the quality of education has focused increasingly on the core subjects, and the comparative performance of schools has been assessed in terms of results in English, mathematics and science, rather than in any of the foundation subjects. The same trend is evident in the most recent reforms in teacher education and the moves towards benchmarking. Furthermore, the current reforms of the National Curriculum start with a clear government directive that the main emphasis should be on making more time available for the development of literacy and numeracy. The danger is that this time will have to be bought at the expense of subjects like music and art. At best, expediency masquerading as thought could lead to their being combined into some ill-conceived amalgam under a broad title such as 'the creative and expressive arts'. Alternatively, we could find one art being pitted against another in a fight for time within an option block. Worst of all, they could be jettisoned entirely from any legal entitlement.

At the time of writing, ministers and spokesmen for OFSTED and QCA are strong on generalities but shift the buck uncomfortably between them when asked for detail. As a result, the feeling of 'uncertainty and unease' that Plummeridge (1991) identified amongst music educators almost ten years ago is now probably stronger than ever. The situation is not new, as several commentators have shown (Reid 1979, Reimer 1970, Temmerman 1991). If music is to retain its status and withstand the fluctuations in thinking – nationally, locally and within individual institutions – those concerned in teaching and organising it must have a clearly-articulated rationale that gives unequivocal answers to the questions of why, when and how music should be taught.

In this chapter we will focus on the first of those questions. The arguments in support of music education fall into two broad categories: those which focus on its utilitarian value and those which emphasise its intrinsic value. Below are some of the main points which can be made under each of these headings.

THE UTILITARIAN VALUE OF MUSIC

Music as vehicle for the transmission of culture

One of the earliest functions of songs and rituals was to record stories of heroism and conquest which encapsulated the religious beliefs of a particular group of people. By teaching these songs to each new generation, the cultural heritage of the society was perpetuated. (Bergethon, Meske and Montgomery 1986; Temmerman 1991).

The role of music in contributing to children's understanding of their culture is still recognised today, although not everybody sees it as the primary purpose. Mills (1991), for example, argues that 'music education has more to do with the education of children than the transmission of some musical heritage.' Ross (1975) and Witkin (1974) are also critical of music education that emphasises ceremony and the conservation of the cultural heritage. Plummeridge (1991), however, argues that these writers fail to appreciate that vocal and instrumental groups can add to the quality of the whole life of a school community and are not solely for the enjoyment and satisfaction of the participants. They reflect the communal feeling in a very real sense. Plummeridge also argues that the works of the great masters, folk songs or hymn tunes are part of that symbolic order which constitutes society. Through them we gain a sense of cultural continuum that gives sense to our society.

The authors of the Calouste Gulbenkian Report (1982) also see the arts as a means of helping schools achieve their function as agencies of cultural education. The meaning of the present and the possibilities of the future can only be grasped, they claim, in the context of what has gone on before. The sense of enduring worth and the sense of excellence and quality can be used to help children formulate and clarify their own ideas and feelings, while developing their personal powers of creative thought and action.

However, they point to several problems implicit in such an approach. There is a need to recognise that the arts are only one aspect of the life of a community. Even within one society there are likely to be several sections, groups or classes, each with its own cultural forms and values. Therefore, to talk of transmitting *the* culture is misleading. It is also important to remember that what is significant in one culture may not be important to another and cultures are constantly changing, evolving and being reappraised. They argue that education needs to help pupils to understand cultural diversity by bringing them into contact with the attitudes, values and institutions of other cultures, as well as exploring their own. It should also emphasise cultural relativity by helping them to recognise and compare their own cultural assumptions and values with these others. Furthermore, it should alert them to the evolutionary nature of their culture and the potential for change, and encourage a cultural perspective by relating contemporary values to the historical forces that mould them.

Music's contribution to social development

Not only does music help individuals relate to the past, it also enables them to relate to their contemporaries. A great deal of music-making involves groups of people performing together. This provides excellent opportunities for individuals of different abilities, ages and social backgrounds to get to know and collaborate with each other. Children who would normally find it difficult to mix can find themselves being valued by their peers for their musical skills (Ben-Tovim 1979). In the process of singing or playing together or composing in groups or ensembles, they learn to take on the roles of both leader and follower (Land and Vaughan 1978). To be successful in either role they have to develop the qualities of cooperation, consideration, responsibility, self-control, self-discipline and leadership (Brocklehurst 1971). Music, therefore, can be an important agent in developing socially well-adjusted individuals.

Music as a form of enjoyment or source of pleasure

One of the signs of being socially well-adjusted is the ability to gain enjoyment from life. One belief, articulated consistently by primary teachers and headteachers, is that music exists within the curriculum 'to give children enjoyment'. In many cases this is seen as its primary purpose and, in some cases, its only purpose. No one would wish to deny the importance of providing children with enjoyable experiences while at school; but, in this context, enjoyment should be a means to an end, not an end in itself. How many teachers would be content to say that the main purpose of language or maths is to produce enjoyment in pupils, although both subjects are equally capable of inducing such a reaction? If providing enjoyable experiences is the main purpose of music, then it has clearly failed. Otherwise why would so few pupils choose to study it after the age of 13 and why have successive studies of children's attitudes to school subjects found music to be so unpopular?

How feasible is it to plan for others' enjoyment? Doting aunts might plan an enjoyable picnic on the beach, only to find that the only recollection the children have is of the discomfort of sand in the sandwiches. A small child given an expensive toy will often gain far more enjoyment from playing with the container or wrapping paper. Is 'enjoyment' an appropriate term for what we experience when we practise repeatedly to get a phrase or rhythm right? Without the pain that such activity often involves, will the ultimate pleasure in performing well ever be felt? Is enjoyment an appropriate or sufficient term to describe the experience of listening to Berg's 'Wozzeck' or a Bartok string quartet, for example? As Swanwick (1979) points out the 'pleasure view of music not only fails to account for some aspects of our musical experiences but also excludes a great deal of the accepted repertoire.' We would also suggest that it plays too readily into the hands of those who would dismiss music as being no more than an unimportant pastime.

Music as education for leisure

Another utilitarian argument which has similar potential for the devaluation of music is that which views music education as education for leisure. The nature of contemporary western society and the trend towards earlier retirement and longer life expectancy has resulted in more people having access to leisure time than in the past. In too many cases, unfortunately, such leisure is enforced. It is often argued that people, whether employed or unemployed, should be helped to use their leisure in a worthwhile way, and one activity usually deemed 'worthwhile' is music. While this may be a good reason for its inclusion in the curriculum, it does present several problems. First, as Plummeridge (1991) has indicated, it reflects a simplistic view of the factors that shape people's lives and determine their leisure pursuits. It also fails to reflect the commitment and seriousness with which many people approach musical pastimes. But most important, as Carlton (1987) and Mills (1991) point out, it reinforces the impression that music is a dispensable luxury to be accommodated outside the curriculum rather than a crucial element within it.

Music's contribution to the preparation of individuals for adult working lives

Lawton (1973) argues that one of the main reasons for establishing state education was to create 'more ability for the labour market', a notion which has been further reinforced of late by the renewed emphasis on vocational education and training. It should not be assumed, however, that a vocational emphasis in the curriculum necessarily militates against the arts or that the arts do not have a role to play in vocational education and training.

The music industry is responsible for a considerable proportion of the gross national product. Recent research conducted by the University of Westminster (1996) on behalf of the Music Education Council indicated that in 1995 the music sector in the UK generated the equivalent of 115,200 full-time jobs; the value of the sector to the UK economy, the sector's 'value added', was estimated to be £2.5 billion; and that the music industry is of a similar size to industries such as water supply, and larger than organic and inorganic chemicals, electric motors, electronic components and shipbuilding. In addition, music is closely linked with a series of 'peripheral' sectors such as broadcasting, the advertising and film industry, the merchandising of goods associated with performers and the specialist music press.

Furthermore, many qualities required by employers can be developed through music. This was particularly well illustrated by Hancox (1982), who describes the experiences of a group of teachers seconded to the Understanding British Industry Project. These teachers identified nine of the major qualities sought by employers and came to the conclusion that most of these could be found in music education: flexibility and adaptability; motor skills; self-awareness and confidence; cooperation; the ability to marshal relevant information to make a decision; and the ability to use initiative.

Music's contribution to individuals' general scholastic development

The emphasis on equipping individuals with the knowledge and skills to contribute to the economic growth of the country has usually led to the highlighting of the core subjects, but it should not be forgotten that music also has a contribution to make here.

It has been a long-held belief that involvement in music can stimulate general intellectual development. Plato stressed music's intellectual value because of the mathematical relationships that Pythagoras discovered within it (Hermann 1965, Naumann, cited by Durrant and Welch 1995). This in turn influenced Renaissance theorists who saw music as a means of training the mind in abstract thinking (Temmerman 1991). Dalcroze, the nineteenth-century Swiss educator, claimed that his system of *eurhythmics* helped children develop general capabilities of observation, apperception, analysis, understanding and memorising, and enabled them to develop more responsive, flexible, vital personalities. A series of experiments conducted in Hungary in the 1970s suggested that music education based on the Kodály method (see Chapter 9) improved performance in general intellectual and physical activities, and also helped social development (Bentley 1975). Further support for this was provided by Kalmar (1982).

In this country, similar benefits of involvement in music and the arts have been highlighted by government reports such as the Hadow Report (1926) and the DES report, *Primary Education in England* (1978). Interest in this revived in 1996 with the publication of research which identified a link between musical ability and mathematical ability, findings which have prompted the Music Industries Association to fund further research into the subject.

All this suggests that, if we are in earnest about raising standards in the core subjects, we should not neglect children's musical education. This is further reinforced when we consider the relationship between music and language development. Music has an important contribution to make to children's language development, particularly in the areas of listening, speaking and reading. In the case of **listening**, a carefully planned music education programme in the early years can help to identify hearing problems and enable children to overcome them by working with such raw materials as pitch, duration, intensity, timbre and rhythm (Wisbey 1980). Through involvement in music, they can be helped to listen with discrimination and sensitivity. This in turn helps them interpret speech and other ways of using language, for example, through poetry, drama and role play (Paynter 1982).

Music's contribution to **speech development** comes from the opportunities it provides for exercising and learning to control the instruments of speech and making the voice more modulated, varied and expressive. This was recognised by the Romans who saw music as an important element in the development of oratory (Taylor 1979). Some people have also been known to alleviate the worst aspects of a stammer by imagining themselves singing when they speak.

Music helps provide children with essential preparatory skills for **reading** by developing their ability to make fine aural discriminations between sounds; providing a wide range of sound patterns; providing experience of decoding and helping to develop left to right orientation (DES 1978; Paynter 1982). In their experiments, Bryant and Bradley (1985) found that children's reading could be improved by teaching them to rhyme and alliterate. They used pictures to do this but, as Mills (1991) argues, the same effects could be produced by drawing attention to the rhymes in song lyrics. In view of all these advantages, it is amazing to find how few schools recognise music as an essential element in their language development programmes. That so little emphasis should have been placed on it in the recently launched national literacy programme is, to say the least, surprising.

Music's contribution to children's physical development

Music also has an undoubted contribution to make to physical development. Through action songs, singing games, rhythm work, striking, plucking, bowing or blowing an instrument at a precise moment in time in a predetermined manner, children develop coordination – both mental and physical – and fine motor skills; attributes that are increasingly important in a computerised world. It was interesting to learn recently, for example, that an unsuccessful candidate for a pilot-training programme had been advised to take up a musical instrument in order to improve his coordination.

Some of the beneficial effects on physical development attributed to music have been rather more bizarre. Theophrastus (c.370–c.288 BC) claimed, for example, that the sound of the flute cured epilepsy and sciatic gout, while Aulus Gellius (c. AD 130–c.180) recommended it as a cure for a snake bite. There is, however, considerable evidence to suggest that singing and the playing of wind instruments can assist respiratory development through the development of good posture, increased lung capacity and diaphragmatic control. 'It doth strengthen all parts of the brest and open the pipes', wrote William Byrd, the seventeenth-century composer. It is probably because of this that so many asthmatics claim to have been helped to overcome some of their worst symptoms by singing and playing wind instruments. Wind instruments can also help overcome problems of defective speech; playing woodwind develops musculature in the lips and cheeks while playing brass involves rhythmic articulation of the tongue.

Taking part in music can benefit a physically awkward, arhythmic child by relaxing muscular tension. Such relaxation can also help change people's moods. Odam (1995) suggests that the recognition of the physical effects of music lies at the heart of the Biblical story of Saul, the categorisation of scales by the Ancient Greeks and the relation of moods to scales in European folk music and in Indian music. Such thinking certainly lies at the basis of much of the work of music therapists. Music can also help children with visual and aural handicaps, as Brocklehurst (1971) and Cleall (1968), among others, have indicated.

It is clear, therefore, that music has a major contribution to make to the development of a healthy mind in a healthy body. Allied to this is the role that it can play in the moral and spiritual development of individuals.

Music's contribution to moral and spiritual development

For Plato, music was 'a moral law' (Davies 1971) and the main objective of music education was the development of the soul's innate capacity for good. This Ancient Greek belief in the ability of music to influence the hearers' emotions and morals (Weiss and Tarskin 1984) continued to hold sway in the Medieval and Renaissance periods, and was also reflected in the views of Comenius in the seventeenth century and Pestalozzi, Froebel, Spencer and Dewey in the nineteenth and early twentieth centuries (Mark 1982, cited in Temmerman 1991; Paynter 1982). In Victorian Britain, music was seen by many as being morally beneficial (Plummeridge 1991) and a means of promoting spirituality (Durrant and Welch 1995). Similar views have also been reflected in other cultures, as Okafor (1989) and Temmerman (1991) have demonstrated in relation to Nigeria and Australia.

In the last few years, with the advent of OFSTED, there has been a revival of interest in such thinking. Schools are now required to demonstrate how they plan for the spiritual, moral, social and cultural development of pupils. As the OFSTED guidance for inspectors shows (OFSTED 1995) music is seen to have an important role to play in this.

THE INTRINSIC VALUE OF MUSIC

The arguments presented so far have focused on the utilitarian value of music education. While these can add weight to the case for the inclusion of music in the curriculum, the advantages are not unique to the subject. It could be argued, for example, that children's social and physical development could be developed just as well through Physical Education (PE); that their linguistic development can be catered for more directly and effectively through English and Drama; and that the best medium for their moral development is a programme of personal and social education.

If music is to have an incontrovertible right to be included in the curriculum, it is important to identify what experiences are unique to it and cannot be made available via other subjects.

Music as an element in being human

One argument for the inclusion of music in the curriculum is that it is a part of the uniqueness of being human (Sachs, 1943; Pratt and Stephens (ed.) 1995, Durrant and Welch 1995). This is reflected in the importance which has been attached to it historically, for example in the education systems of the Ancient Greeks, the Romans, the Medieval and Renaissance periods and in the education reforms of the nineteenth century (Taylor 1979). It has also formed a valued part of traditional education in India and China; 'music', said Confucius, 'affords a kind of pleasure which human beings cannot do without' (Baker 1975). Its importance is clearly recognised in the education systems of a wide variety of contemporary societies. In this country, even before music became a compulsory part of the curriculum, most schools made some attempt – however limited – to give at least some children access to music. Today, schools which are not subject to the National Curriculum still place considerable emphasis on music, as a glance through the pages of any directory of public schools will show.

Focusing specifically on young children, most toy shops sell musical instruments (often of a poor quality, unfortunately), together with tapes of music for listening. Music is also included in the radio and television programmes for very young children and their parents. All cultures also have a wealth of traditional nursery songs and musical games, which again suggests that music is a central element of being human. If this is so, and if education exists in order to help make us human, then music must be an indispensable part of the process.

Music as a language

Another argument that focuses on the intrinsic value of music is concerned with the notion of its being a language. This perception is repeatedly encountered in publications on music education, in general conversations with teachers and in the policy statements of schools. In practice, it is reflected in such activities as asking children to describe 'what a piece of music is about' or to decide whether a tune is 'happy' or 'sad'. It is, however, a highly contentious notion. A language, it may be argued, must have a vocabulary with agreed meanings, capable of being defined in a dictionary. Suzanne Langer (1957) rejects the notion that music can be a language in this sense, as does Hindemith (1952). Scrimshaw (1974) further argues that a language must have syntactical rules, must be translatable and any statement which it makes must be capable of negation; requirements that music does not fulfil.

Deryck Cooke (1959), on the other hand, argues that music is a language. He analyses particular melodic patterns and intervals in the major, minor and chromatic scales and assigns specific meanings to them. The referent for a major third, for example, is 'joy'. For a minor second it is 'spiritless anguish', while a sharp fourth represents 'devilish and inimical forces'. Cooke argues that, through the use of these translations, the knowledgeable listener can participate in music's meaning. To a certain extent, this reflects the approach taken by Schweitzer (1952) in his analysis of Bach's works. There, particular types of motifs and melodic progression are viewed as representations of specific ideas, such as weeping or resurrection and ascension. Cooke focuses specifically on tonal music, but the same approach could presumably be applied to other musical styles, given sufficient experience of them and acclimatisation to their conventions.

In *A Basis for Music Education* (1979), Keith Swanwick describes an experiment to try to identify external referents for music. He devised simple tonal elements with two parts to them: a 'basic unit', which establishes the stylistic 'norm', and an 'event', which represents a departure from the norm. For example, a basic unit might consist of two pitches repeated regularly on a crotchet beat, while the event occurs when the same notes are played as quavers. Using the technique of the Semantic Differential, the listener was asked to decide where the event lay on a seven-point progression on a continuum; for example, did it incline towards 'active' rather than 'passive' or towards 'inward-looking' rather than 'outward-looking' and how closely did it incline to a particular end of the continuum? For 7–9 year pupils, pictures were used instead of words and the points on each continuum were reduced to five. Analysis of the results for over 300 subjects led Swanwick to the conclusion that music does have meaning when people really attend to it and when they understand the norms within which it operates.

Swanwick's experiment was based on small units of music. While it might be possible to find agreement on meaning in those contexts, it does not follow that the same would hold true if longer sections or whole pieces of music were involved. The experiences of Francesco Berger (Scholes 1972, p.835) suggest the opposite. Berger described how he once wrote a piano piece that was meant to represent the discovery by Pharaoh's daughter of Moses in the bulrushes. He played it to three fellow composers and asked them to describe what it meant to them. One thought it represented 'daybreak as seen from the lowest gallery of a Welsh coal mine'; the second thought it represented 'a boar-hunt in Russia' while, for the third, it represented 'an enamoured couple whispering love vows'. These composers were presumably well-versed in the norms within which the music operated and were well acclimatised to its conventions and context, yet they could not agree on the meaning of the music. Swanwick himself warns against taking a simplistic view of music as 'a kind of communication code between composer and listener', and he develops his argument to trace the complexities of the interplay between composer, the music, the listener and the performer.

Hirst (1974) suggests that too much emphasis has been placed on naming and reference as central elements in language. Meaning and understanding do not depend on dictionary definitions but derive from the use made of language in particular contexts. This view has been further developed by Aspin (1984) who argues that, where there is shared contextual meaning, sounds, signs, gestures and movements can also have significance; meaning does not have to be confined to words. Plummeridge (1991) illustrates this with reference to a football match. The actions of a player have meaning for someone who understands the game in a way that it cannot for someone who does not understand the context and cannot 'read' the movements. Similarly, in a composition or improvisation activity, particular sounds can be 'right', 'wrong', 'effective' or 'weak' in specific contexts, and when people make decisions and act on the basis of how the sounds appear in these contexts they are displaying 'musical understanding'. What remains unclear, however, is the extent to which Hirst and Plummeridge see such meanings as being entirely a function of their context and to what extent they could be transferred to other contexts. What is clear from this is that the notion of music as a language is a far more complex issue than is often realised.

Music as the expression of emotion

Another contentious issue concerns the relationship between music and emotion. It can be argued that there are two aspects to human life: the external world that exists independently of the individual, and the internal world which can only exist while the individual exists. This is the world of the feelings and the emotions. Some have argued that it is possible to transmit these emotions to others through art. For Tolstoy, for example, the best work of art is one which transmits a powerfully felt, clearly-defined emotion in a direct and unambiguous way from the artist to the recipient. In his case, the emotion also had to be good and had to lead to Christian brotherhood.

This approach raises several problems. First, if what artists are trying to do is to convey their emotions, why do they not simply give vent to them directly? If they are feeling angry, why do they not simply scream and shout and wave their fists at an audience? If they wanted to express their rage to far more people than can be crammed into a concert hall, they could produce a video or a film or appear on a broadcast. If they wanted to present their emotion in any form other than direct physical vocalisation or movement, they would probably be best advised to communicate their anger in writing. In certain circumstances it might be more expedient to use a more equivocal medium, in the way that tunes and visual symbols

have been used to relay messages and maintain solidarity in the face of
political or religious persecution. In most cases, however, a well-crafted
letter or article would probably be the best way of giving vent to an emotion. But how often have people sat down to write letters of complaint or
articles lampooning a particular piece of bureaucratic folly only to find that
that they lose momentum before the end? The process of writing has
helped them 'work it out of their system' and they cannot sustain the emotion any further.

Given this situation, is there any reason to suppose that a composer can
sustain an emotion for the probably far longer period of time needed to
produce a piece of music? Langer (1957) argues that an artist need not be
in a personal state of despair to be able to produce a tragedy. Nobody
could work in such a state of mind. They would be too preoccupied with
their thoughts to be able to focus on anything else. The fact that composers
often work at the same time on several works with widely differing moods
also believes the notion that an art work is a direct transmission of emotions,
unless of course such artists are particularly volatile. Even in producing
the most joyful piece of music, a composer might experience extreme
frustration and anger at not being able to get a particular section to sound
right.

This suggests therefore that the relationship between emotions and art
works are more complex than such writers as Tolstoy have claimed. Dewey
(1958) has argued that the types of emotions expressed in the arts of painting and music are distinctive and cannot be expressed in words. This
echoes Heine's statement: 'Where words leave off there music does begin'.
Drawing on the work of Dewey and Langer particularly, Reimer (1970)
presents a very interesting and coherent theory of the interrelationship
between art and feeling. The whole of human life, he argues, is saturated
with feeling. Any attempts to categorise these feelings only emphasises
their complexity. As an example he takes the word 'love'. This one word is
incapable of encapsulating the breadth of subtle, varied and complex emotions which fall within that category. If the word is qualified and we talk
about 'parental love', 'romantic love' and so on, the situation becomes
even more complex because each new category involves additional realms
of feeling. A further difficulty arises from the indistinctness of feelings and
the overlap between them, so that 'hate', for example might also involve
elements of 'fear'.

To overcome such problems, Reimer applies the term 'emotions' to the
'category words' and the term 'feeling' to the subjective reality. Feeling
itself cannot be named because, as we have already seen, the category
words are limited. The forms of art, however, enable us to receive an experience of feeling and to refine and deepen those experiences in the way that
words cannot. This could be taken further to say that, because sounds are
more abstract than the materials of the other art forms, music is even more

important as a means of experiencing feelings. If so, this must be one of the strongest reasons for its inclusion in the curriculum.

DEVELOPING A RATIONALE IN CONTEXT

Whether they focus on utilitarian or intrinsic values, arguments in support of a subject cannot be presented in isolation. They will need to take account of the perceived purpose of education in general. If the main purpose of education is seen as a preparation for adult life, then music education, if it is to be justified as education, will need to reflect this principle in some way (Plummeridge 1991). However, fashions in what is viewed as important in education change and this has an impact on what is considered important within particular subjects. Rainbow (1968) points to the way that 'at one time school music has been supported chiefly for its usefulness as an enhancement of divine service; at other times its very uselessness has been acclaimed as its chief virtue.' Land and Vaughan (1978) and Temmerman (1991) have traced similar fluctuations in fashion in America and Australia.

With the advent of local management of schools (LMS), the picture has been complicated, and differing views of what is or is not important in education can exist within one authority, town or neighbourhood. The governors of one school might see education for leisure as a significant aspect of education while governors of a neighbouring school might see preparation for the world of work as all-important. The senior management of one school might see music as an activity for the talented few while in another school 'music for all' is the catchphrase. One headteacher might see a musical production as primarily a good marketing ploy while another will see it as a valuable experience in itself.

Anyone presenting the case for music education will need to be aware of the prevailing opinion locally and tailor the arguments accordingly. It might even be necessary to give greater emphasis to one argument in order to protect the subject and to secure the focus on other values. This might sound like a recipe for schizophrenia. To prevent this, it is essential to differentiate between what is ultimately valuable and what needs to be emphasised for short-term tactical purposes. The means must not be allowed to detract from the ends. It is also important to be clear about our thinking, so that we can identify when one set of interests might be militating against another. For example, an over-concern with presenting high profile concerts for marketing purposes could lead to the erosion of the experiences offered in the classroom for the majority of pupils.

As Land and Vaughan (1978) point out, musical and non-musical goals can be used together effectively, so long as the teacher realises which is being used and uses both in proper balance to assist students' musical growth.

It might be claimed that all these arguments are rather high-faluting and removed from the realities of the early years classroom. We make no excuses for this. Whatever is taught in the early years must be placed in a wider context. The child playing with water and differentiating between objects which float and sink is starting on a road which could lead her eventually to design an ocean going vessel. The child sitting under a suspended cymbal and enjoying the feel of the vibrations around him might one day become a composer. The wider our perspective on the education process in general, the better focused will be our particular contribution to that process.

Chapter 2

The focus of music education

TRADITIONAL SITUATION

Up until the late 1960s and early 1970s, the main focus for music education in this country was performance – particularly instrumental
performance – backed up by training in theory and the history of music.
The staple fare was Western Music, usually of the Baroque, Classical and
Romantic periods. There was little emphasis on composition, although
universities turned out graduates who could forge a five-part fugue in the
style of Bach at the drop of a hat. Improvisation was largely confined to
the organ loft, where performers were equipped with enough mix-and-
match clichés to cover up delays in delivering the offertory, coffin or the
bride.

CHANGING PERCEPTIONS

Towards the end of the 1960s, some publications emerged that challenged
these assumptions and drew attention to the value of exploring twentieth-
century and Early Music and involving students in making their own
music, rather than listening to that of others. Possibly because these
approaches were allied to the 'avant garde' movement, there was a tendency for their proponents to overstate their case, drawing an
unnecessarily vehement backlash from traditionalists. At the time, there
were no national guidelines and precious few local guidelines on music
education. Notions of continuity and progression were far from fashion-
able, the emphasis being on the autonomy of the class teacher. As a result,
it was not unusual to find teachers in the same school espousing widely
differing viewpoints, so that the experiences which their pupils received
lacked development, coherence or direction. This was particularly the
case in the early years of secondary school. At later points the demands of
the external examination boards dictated largely what was done,
although there was also considerable difference of emphasis between
some boards. At primary level, it was very much a hit or miss affair

whether children received any music at all. Even in schools which did provide for the subject, there was rarely much evidence of coherence, continuity and development.

THE PARAMETERS OF MUSIC

It was the publication of *A Basis of Music Education* by Keith Swanwick (1979) which helped show a way out of this morass. This book challenged many assumptions, cleared up many confusions, brought together approaches which had become needlessly polarised and welded them into a coherent view of music education that was applicable across all phases. Swanwick identified three main ways in which people can become directly involved in music: composition, audition and performance. By the term 'audition', he meant attending to music as an audience (not necessarily in a concert hall) and becoming involved in its contemplation. All three activities, he argued, should be central to music education at every level. Although separate, they were not to be divorced entirely from each other. Performers, for example, must listen very carefully if they are to be successful and composers make use of listening and performing while creating new works. Therefore, within teaching and learning programmes, the three activities should be interrelated. Musical skills and theoretical and historical information were important only as a means of supporting the three main activities and not as ends in themselves; a difficult concept for many teachers whose raison d'être seemed to be founded on their mastery of scales, arpeggios and how to decipher acciacaturas.

Swanwick's so-called CLASP model met with a mixed reception. There were those who saw it as a way forward, while others dismissed it as yet another fad. During the 1980s, however, its influence was clearly seen in two highly significant documents published by the DES, 'Music 5–14' and later 'Music 5–16'. The latter, which appeared in 1985, was the fourth in the *Curriculum Matters Series*, produced by HMI as 'a framework within which schools might develop a music programme appropriate to its own pupils.' By the time the final stage of consultation on the document had been reached in 1987, plans to establish a National Curriculum had been announced.

The nature and content of the National Curriculum changed considerably during its evolution. By the time the interim report for Music was published in December 1990, it had been decided that children would only be given externally set tests in English, mathematics and science, and that music was to be a compulsory subject only up to the age of 14. In their original form the Attainment Targets for music were Performing, Composing and Appraising, corresponding to the three main parameters of Swanwick's model. This format was accepted in Wales. The consultation process in England, however, ran far less smoothly, mainly because Kenneth Clarke, the then Secretary of State for Education, was determined to reduce the number of Attainment Targets to two, in the hope that shortening the document would make it easier to understand. However, what he had failed to anticipate was the degree of support that the original document would receive from teachers. Eventually a compromise was suggested. Although there were two Attainment Targets (Listening and Appraising, Composing and Performing), the second was to be given twice as much weighting as the first in any guidance on assessment. In the event, this weighting was not actually included in either the 1992 Order for England or in the revised Order of 1995, although such a weighting, according to Pratt and Stephens (1995) 'is clearly implied by the content and layout of the curriculum.'

Despite these machinations, two important developments had taken place. For the first time since the 1870 Act, every child between the ages of 5 and 14 had a legal right to be taught music, and there was now agreement nationally that music education should be based on principles very similar to those articulated by Swanwick in 1979. These same principles were retained in the 1994 Dearing revision of the National Curriculum and will no doubt influence the next version to be launched in the new millennium.

THE ELEMENTS OF MUSIC

One of the features of the Dearing revision was the renewed emphasis which it placed on the elements of music. These can be classified as:

- Pitch;
- Duration (including Beat, Accent, Rhythm and Metre);
- Tempo or pace;
- Timbre or Tone Colour;
- Texture;
- Dynamics;
- Structure;
- Silence.

Through involvement in composing, performing, listening and appraising activities, children develop familiarity with these concepts, the facility to identify them in the work of others, and the ability to apply them to their own work.

The 1994 version of the National Curriculum indicates what our final goal should be in developing a grasp of each of these concepts but gives very little indication of what sequence of activities could help us reach that goal and what interim stages there might be in the process. It is rather like being told that you have to go to Cairo without being given any indication of which bus to take to which local station, which airport to aim for or which flight to take. In Chapter 12, we shall try to compensate for this by identifying stages through which children can be helped towards the final goal. We do not pretend that those stages are incontrovertible. They should be viewed as an attempt to contribute to what Pratt and Stephens (1995) have identified as a need to 'unwrap' the terse descriptions in the Dearing documentation.

STYLES OF MUSIC

One thing that is clear from the 1994 version of the National Curriculum, and which was emphasised at each stage prior to that, is that children's command of the musical elements of music should be developed through experience of compositions from a wide range of styles, cultures and historical origins. It is important, therefore, that from the early years on, the music presented in schools should reflect this diversity. Thus, for example, children can be given the opportunity to develop the notion of beat by singing African or Afro-Caribbean folk songs, to make up their own tunes using the notes of an Indian scale or to hear the varied timbres produced by orchestral and jazz trumpeters. This is important for all schools in every part of the country.

Schools in areas with a rich ethnic mix are very fortunate in that their pupils will have access to an additional wealth of songs, rhymes and nursery and playground games that they have learnt at home from their parents and grandparents. Many schools in such areas have also benefited considerably from inviting parents, relatives and representatives of the community to come and tell stories, sing and perform to their pupils. Through sharing a diversity of experiences children are helped to appreciate not only the differences but also the underlying similarities between the different musical and cultural experiences.

Where the range of music in the local community is less diverse, schools will need to rely more heavily on recorded and published material. Luckily, most musical courses and resource materials do represent a range of musical styles and cultures to help with this process, and reference is made to some of these in the section on resources.

TEACHING *THROUGH* MUSIC

The emphasis in the National Curriculum and in this book centres very much on the teaching *of* music. This is not to say that schools cannot also teach *through* music. The use of songs to help children to grasp concepts of number, colours, days of the week, months of the year and so on is an important aspect of many cultures and due regard must be paid to this. Having said that, it must be emphasised that simply using songs in this way does not necessarily indicate a contribution to children's musical development. For this to happen, the teacher will need to focus on such aspects as the accuracy of pitching, rhythm and phrasing and to plan explicitly for the development, application or reinforcement of relevant skills.

The remainder of this book will be devoted to such concerns. First, however, it will be useful to identify what young children bring with them to school and what we know about the patterns of their early musical development.

Chapter 3

Identifying the starting point – children's pre-school and home musical experiences

PRIOR EXPERIENCE AND PLANNING WORK

No two children starting school will have had the same experiences. Some children come from homes where there are large numbers of books and where parents and other adults tell stories and read to them regularly. Others might have very limited contact with books and rarely engage in extended conversation with an adult. One child might have been taught to name colours, to count, to identify letters and numbers, while another will have had none of these opportunities. The musical experiences made available to children will also differ from one home to another. Some children might have been taught a range of songs and nursery rhymes, might be sung to daily, have instruments around them, hear music being played regularly and have their own collection of tapes and CDs. Others' encounters with music might have included none of these experiences.

In planning work in English and mathematics, nursery and infant teachers are usually very aware of differences in children's prior experiences and make considerable efforts to adapt their planning accordingly. The same is less evident in music. Too often, children in a music class are treated as if they were all at the same starting point. Thus, some children spend a great deal of time revisiting old ground while others are denied the opportunity to compensate for lack of previous experiences. This applies not only to infant classes. Too often, junior and even secondary pupils are fed an undifferentiated diet, despite tremendous differences in their interests, experiences and abilities.

If we are to provide effectively for children's musical growth, we need to be aware of some of the patterns of development which they can be expected to have followed before coming to school, so that a preliminary picture can be established. We also need to acquaint ourselves with the likely impact of home and school experiences on musical growth and devise ways of recording and using this information to help us in our planning.

ANTENATAL MUSICAL EXPERIENCES

Anecdotal and research evidence suggests that the unborn foetus reacts to music. Expectant mothers often describe how they can feel more movement in the womb when they listen to music. Ostwald (1973) reported that, in the case of pregnant performers, the pattern varies. Singers found that the unborn child seemed quieter when they were performing. Instrumentalists, on the other hand, found that the foetus became more active during or shortly after a performance. Whether this has an effect on the future musical development of the child is unknown. We do not even know whether the movement, when it occurs, is evidence that the unborn baby can actually hear in the womb or whether the movement is sparked by some chemical reaction set up in the mother as she listens or performs.

EXPERIENCES AT BIRTH

What we do know is that the sound a baby makes at birth is very significant; the first cry has been imbued with significance in a range of cultures. For Shakespeare's 'King Lear' (Act IV, Scene 6), it is evidence of immediate recognition of the sorrows of the world, a sentiment which echoes Lucretius's remark that 'The wailing of the new-born infant is mingled with the dirge for the dead.' For Montessori (1936) it is the cry of 'a pilgrim who comes from somewhere far distant, worn out and wounded'. Margaret Mead (1964) describes how, in the Manus Tribe, a nurse is at hand to echo the child's first cry so that the baby has an immediate response to the sound that it makes. Later the mother helps the child to sleep by crying in tune with the child's cry, but louder.

EARLY INFANCY

From birth onwards children have access to a vast array of music. In Western cultures this includes rattles, musical toys, tapes of nursery rhymes and songs and the other paraphernalia of the baby industry. It might also include live performance of nursery rhymes, lullabies and other songs to help soothe and comfort, although there is increasing complaint about the reluctance of parents to sing to their offspring (for example, Carlton 1987). Even if they do not have access to live music-making or have few opportunities to play with musical instruments, most children will hear a wide range of music on the radio, television, on tapes and CDs and as background 'muzak' in supermarkets, department stores, railway stations and so on. Some have argued that the plethora of music available is in danger of dulling children's reactions; but this is rather like saying that children are surrounded by too many visual experiences. Children do not become blind by being surrounded by exciting sights. They select areas of focus and interest and relate these to other contrasting and parallel experiences. There is no reason to suppose that they do not do the same when they are listening.

MOOG'S STUDY

A highly influential study of early musical development was conducted in Germany by Helmut Moog (1976). Moog investigated the stages in the musical development of children aged 0–5 years. Eight thousand individual tests were carried out with nearly 500 children, and the observations of approximately 1,000 parents were evaluated. The children were left to their own devices, with no explicit attempt being made to intervene in their musical progress. The general sequence of musical development identified from the results is summarised in Table 3.1. As with any study of the type, however, the conclusions should be approached with caution, especially where ages are concerned. Those quoted are average ages and should not be used as indicators of retarded development or as a reason to delay giving children particular types of experiences until they are 'ready' for them.

THE EFFECT OF HOME EXPERIENCES ON CHILDREN'S MUSICAL DEVELOPMENT

To what extent children's home experiences influence their musical development is difficult to determine. In Moog's study, this influence only began to become apparent when the child reached the age of 3, but others have suggested that the effects become apparent at an earlier stage. Part of the problem lies in the organisation of the studies. Parents who agree to take part in an investigation of musical development might place far more emphasis on music than they would do normally, which could affect the results. Another problem is that there is no guarantee that because a relationship is found between home background and a child's musical development in the early years, the same relationship will continue to hold true as the child grows older.

Some studies have drawn on individuals' memories of the musical environment in which they were brought up. The reliability of such memories can be questionable and there is a danger that only the most memorable or dramatic aspects of the childhood environment are highlighted, with the result that any relationship patterns established may be distortions of the real situation.

Schuter-Dyson and Gabriel (1981) present a detailed account of a number of studies of the relationship between home background and children's musical development. They conclude that 'a musically-stimulating home is certainly likely to help children to make the best of whatever potential they may possess. Whether the parents play or sing is especially

Table 3.1 A summary of Moog's conclusions on the general sequence of musical development in young children

Age	Musical responses		Vocal responses
	Through movement		
1st few weeks	Muscular contractions in response to sudden loud noises.		
c. time of first smile	Music no longer arouses but has calming effect. High-pitched voices and instruments more soothing than low pitched sounds.		
2–3 mths			Babbling in preparation for speech begins. Elicited by speaking to child.
3–6 mths	Turns towards source. Shows expressions, e.g. astonishment or pleasure.		
6 mths	Stops still and concentrates on music when it is played. Begins to respond with very clear repetitive whole body movements, e.g. sways from side to side or bouncing up and down motor movements. Movement response strongest in relation to beautiful tone, not the rhythm. Seems first to enjoy music for *sounds* not rhythms or words. Selects sensuously beautiful sound.		
7–8 mths			Babbling songs elicited by singing or playing music to child. Babbling songs not diatonic; very wide range; microtones used.
9–12 mths	Marked extension of response via movements, songs and utterances		
12 mths			Only very few can produce songs resembling something sung to them. Words/parts of words imitated not rhythm or pitch.

Table 3.1 – contd

Age	Through movement	Vocal responses
12–18 mths	Size, strength and variety of movements increases.	Increasing ability to sing. Increase in spontaneous singing.
18 mths	Some begin to try to perform movements with others. Beginning of social behaviour in movement to music.	
18 mths–2 yrs	Begins, for short stretches, to match movements to rhythm of the music.	Rhythm as well as sound of words begin to be reproduced. Similarity of pitch also increases. Progression from singing short phrases to singing longer songs. Songs still non-diatonic, making use of microtones. Rhythmically simple.
2–3 yrs	Concentrated, still, attentive listening begins to appear for short periods of c.5 mins. Sometimes prefers to respond thus than through movement. Number of overall movement responses to music falls but considerable increase in *variety* of movement and no. of *coordinated movements* increases.	Marked increase in amount of singing. Children sing to themselves and do not expect response, beyond being complimented possibly. They sing more and for longer periods. Songs include those learnt and those made up spontaneously.
	At first, cannot keep time to music heard but *can* keep time to own spontaneous songs. At first can only do so for short stretches of time but gradually can do so for longer.	Increase in number and length of songs particularly apparent in spontaneous songs.
	Spectacular progress in use of space when moving.	Less variety in rhythm of spontaneous songs than in past but some form of structure apparent.
		Can imitate at least part of a song sung to them. More likely at first to be able to imitate words and rhythms than to imitate pitch. Reacts to rhythm when combined with words but not necessarily to pure rhythm divorced from words.
		In addition to imitative and spontaneous songs, children produce *pot pourri* songs i.e. spontaneous songs made up of fragments of learnt songs.

Age	Through movement	Vocal responses
		Development of imitative singing depends more on child's environment than at an earlier stage. Effects of nursery school seen. Children with largest repertoire came from homes where parents sang particularly often.
3 yrs		Average vocal range = 1st octave of treble clef.
3–4 yrs	Total number of movements to music decline still further. Coordination between movement and ms remains same but *variety* of movements increases still further. Simultaneous movements observed. Children dance mainly on their own.	No. and scope of songs begin to increase. These include spontaneous, imitative and *imaginative songs* i.e. partly spontaneous and partly snatches which they know or new versions of these.
	Some show wish for social dancing after they have been introduced to it.	Great extension of *pot pourri songs.*
	Most can distinguish between fast and slow.	Also develop *narrative songs* where any words are sung, so long as they tell a story.
	Differences in home environment begin to show effect in terms of songs and games which children are taught at home.	
4–6 yrs	Progress in keeping movements in time with music. Can keep time for longer periods than previously. Movements of parts of the body in time to music far more frequent than movements of the whole body. In accompanying own singing, sometimes claps rhythm of words.	Spontaneous songs continue. Pot-pourri songs less frequent than at earlier stage.
		Make up words/tunes more often than at earlier stage.
	Movements made to own singing far better coordinated than those made to music heard. Some able to alter movements with tempo. Some altered MVOs with dynamic range.	In reproducing learned songs, mistakes in words and rhythm less frequent than out-of-tune singing.

important, and the availability of an instrument seems especially important.' They go on to point out that 'parents who do not perform can
encourage their children to sing with recordings or broadcasts and to listen
to a wide range of music, thus providing a richer environment than would
have been possible in earlier times' (p.210).

More recently, Howe and Sloboda (1991a, 1991b) have reported the qualitative findings of an interview study of 42 successful child musicians, in
which they and their parents were asked about significant influences on
their early musical development. The only general statement that could be
drawn from these studies was that there is no one route to musical excellence. Each student's route is unique to that particular person.
Nevertheless, a vital element seemed to be the long-term commitment of
parents to providing support for the daily routine of the children's musical
activities, in helping them get the work done; and in providing time, trans-
port, money, organisation and motivation. Most of the parents and children
took frequency of lessons and regularity of practice for granted. However,
the actual impact of practice was difficult to determine. Despite earlier
studies which indicate a strong correlation between amount of practice
and level of performance in adult musicians, Sloboda and Howe suggest
that 'amongst relatively successful child musicians, relationships between
performance and sheer amount of time spent practising may be weak or
non-existent'. Even if these patterns of relationship exist in the case of
gifted musicians, it does not necessarily follow that they will also hold true
for children of average musical ability.

One factor that might be relevant in the studies of the effect of home
background on children's musical growth concerns the sex of the children
involved. In investigations of sibling development a shared home is usually treated as a constant variable. However, this is not necessarily the
case, as the findings of Pugh (1979) suggest. As part of this study, a sample
of 100 boys and girls were asked to indicate on a questionnaire what types
of musical experiences occurred within the home. The responses were
scored on a high–low scale and subjected to quantitative analysis. The
results indicated that boys gave a lower estimation of their home musical
lives than did their female siblings. While this might reflect a difference in
their reactions to the same environment, it might be that parents placed
greater emphasis on music in the presence of their daughters than in the
presence of their sons. Whatever the reason, it points to the need to treat
the results of such studies with care.

BASE-LINE ASSESSMENT

The conclusion to be drawn from the above evidence is that there is no
blueprint for success musically, and that many more studies will have to be
conducted before we can draw any firm conclusions. However, this does

not remove the necessity to try to build a clear picture of the forces at play in the musical experiences of our pupils. This is essential if we are to:

- build on children's experiences and develop them further;
- avoid needless and unproductive repetition of experiences;
- challenge assumptions about what the children do or do not know, and can or cannot do;
- create an accurate view of the extent and rate of progress made by pupils and present them with appropriate challenges to develop further.

One way of doing this is through the use of base-line assessment. In 1996, SCAA produced draft proposals for the production of statutory schemes of base-line assessment to be used by schools to identify the ability of young children starting school in the areas of:

- language and literature;
- mathematics;
- and personal and social education.

Working with parents, both before the child's arrival in school and later, the school will build up a profile of a child's experiences and abilities, based on a series of statements.

Scheme providers – such as local education authorities – may also, if they wish, seek approval to extend the criteria to include other areas of experience. We suggest that Figure 3.1 could be the basis for base-line assessment for music.

Through discussion with parents and observation, the teacher could record the level at which the child is performing on entry to the school. This could be indicated on a 5 point scale (1 Low – 5 High) or a three point scale if that was considered preferable. Using this information, the school could plan for appropriately differentiated activities and set down a basic marker against which the rate and extent of subsequent development can be assessed. While there are undoubted advantages in the use of base-line assessment, there are also potential pitfalls, and teachers will need to guard against the danger of:

- focusing on those who already have had the experiences at the expense of their peers, or vice versa;
- equating experience with ability;
- not recognising that maturation can be at different rates and that a child who might be slower to start can actually outstrip others eventually;
- setting a ceiling on children's ability and challenge because they have not received as much stimulation from home.

There might also be a danger of some parents painting a rosier picture of their home musical environments and their children's abilities, while other more modest parents underestimate these aspects.

Name:					
Date of birth:					
Experiences and ability in music					
Statement	**1**	**2**	**3**	**4**	**5**
Is able to sing a number of songs and/or nursery rhymes					
Is able to sing alone as well as with others					
Is able to identify songs or pieces of music when they are played					
Is able to move in time to music					
Is able to produce sounds on an instrument/instruments					
Is able to sing/play in time with others					
Shows interest in music played					
Is able to talk about favourite pieces of music					

Figure 3.1 Base-line assessment for music to be used at point of entry

In the light of this preliminary information, the school will be able, from the outset, to begin to plan a differentiated programme to help children meet the desired outcomes and attainment targets for early years music.

Chapter 4

Vocal performance

THE VOICE AS AN INSTRUMENT

One of the most important ways of gaining musical understanding is through performing on an instrument. One of the most important instruments is the voice. As we sing, we are directly involved in a complex process of coordination, involving the brain, the ears, the lungs, the diaphragm, the vocal cords, the lips and the teeth. Our bodies become instruments. Moog's findings show that singing is one of the earliest ways in which we take part or react to music. Therefore it is one of the most intimate and elemental of musical experiences. The focus on subtleties of inflection, pitch and tone that singing entails also helps to make the speaking voice a more expressive tool. It is no accident that the training of actors often includes singing lessons and other forms of voice training.

The way in which we sing influences not only vocal music but also the nature of instrumental music. The lengths of phrases in vocal, wind and brass music are determined by the number and the length of notes that we can sing or play comfortably with one breath. This has also influenced music played on very different types of instruments. There is no reason for the phrases in organ, piano or violin music to be divided into phrases because the organ's bellows can keep churning out air at a constant rate all the time that it is switched on, and the length of a pianist's or violinist's phrase need only be constrained by fatigue in the muscles of the fingers, hands and arms. Despite this, however, the phrasing of music for these instruments tends to be similar to that of vocal music. This is one of the reasons why the most sensitive and well coordinated instrumental performances arise when they have been approached through vocal performance, a factor we shall discuss in further detail later. In addition, the voice is portable and cheap – two other factors which must make it attractive to any cash-strapped school.

TEACHING SINGING

Teachers often feel reticent about teaching singing because they feel that their own voices are poor, but a wonderful voice is not always an advantage.

We have known teachers who have been so proud of their vocal prowess and so anxious to preserve it for the termly performance with the local operatic group that they have not dared to use it in class. As with so many other aspects of their work, infant teachers need to make the best use of what they have got. They might not be brilliant painters but they wield a brush knowing that, unless they do so, their charges are unlikely to learn. In the same way, they play ball games, read stories and perform a whole range of activities without for one moment supposing that they must demonstrate professional standards in each of these areas. The professionalism comes from putting whatever skills they have to the best effect as a support to their pupils. The same should be the case with the teaching of singing.

Many teachers worry that they will not be able to teach singing because they cannot play the piano. In fact, the piano can be a major disadvantage to the teaching of singing, particularly with young children. To sing successfully, children need to be able to control their voices and be able to maintain a constant volume on a note. The piano provides a poor example of how to do this since the notes, once struck, quickly die away. A keyboard is more useful because of its ability to maintain a constant volume on a note as well as to produce increases and decreases in sound. But for a piano or keyboard to be of any real help in the classroom, a teacher should be adept at playing it without looking at her hands and be able to play the same tunes in a variety of keys, to match the natural pitches of individual children's voices. Even then, the very size of a piano or keyboard can create a barrier between the teacher and pupils and destroy the intimate environment that is so important in any class, particularly in the early years. The volume of such instruments can also make it difficult for a teacher to gauge precisely what or how individual children are singing. This is made more difficult by the fact that, even with the lightest of keyboards, the teacher has to be fairly static while performing and cannot get close enough to individual children to give extra help or to diagnose problems that they might be experiencing.

The guitar is a far more useful instrument to accompany classroom singing. It is portable, not too loud, and enables the teacher and pupils to work together in close proximity. Even when playing and singing, the teacher can go to a child who might be experiencing difficulty or who needs extra support and give help without drawing undue attention to the individual concerned. With the aid of a capo even a fairly mediocre performer can also adapt a song to a range of pitches appropriate to the vocal ranges of particular pupils.

Whether an instrument is used or not, the most important element in the teaching of vocal work is unaccompanied singing. This enables the children to concentrate on the precise sounds to be copied, without any of the confusion which might arise in trying to differentiate between a melody and its accompaniment. It also enables the teacher to hear more clearly how well individual children are progressing and to be able to provide focused help and support.

TEACHING A SONG BY ROTE

A great deal of music will need to be taught to infant children by rote. This is the equivalent of extending their experiences of written and spoken language through telling stories and reading to them, so that a wealth of experiences is created which will ultimately form the bases for developing knowledge, skills and understanding of specific concepts.

The following approach to the teaching of songs by rote is by no means the only approach that can be used, but it is one which has been used successfully both by ourselves and also by a large number of other teachers. What is presented here is merely an outline, to be adapted to the particular style and circumstances of each teacher. It is adapted from the introduction to Pugh and Pugh 1995.

Introducing the song

It is rarely a good idea to launch into a song without first discussing it, since it can be very confusing for the children. A song might be introduced by first explaining the background to it (for example, that it is a song about winter) or by giving an outline of the story which it contains or by reference to a picture which reflects the content of the song.

The teacher then sings the song through, making sure that it is presented as a story. The use of eye contact, changes of volume and physical and vocal expressions to reflect the content of the words are as important in this context as in the telling of an ordinary story. The use of clear mouth movements is also important since we all rely very much on watching others' mouth shapes when we are trying to work out what they are saying or trying to memorise words for ourselves. Neglecting this aspect can work to the detriment of those children who might have as yet undiagnosed hearing difficulties. It also leads to those colourful mispronunciations which are legion in the history of any infant school. 'Who built the ark? No one No one' might seem an apocryphal mishearing but one to which we can attest.

As with other areas of their experiences, young children enjoy and need repetition if they are to learn. Therefore, the song now needs to be repeated.

When this has been done, the teacher sings the first line of the song, giving the pitch of the first note clearly and counting the children in on that note. The first line is sung several times before the second line is tackled. The two lines are then combined before the third is added. Gradually the learnt lines are repeated with new ones added, until eventually the whole verse has been sung. A three-line verse, for example, might be built up as follows: Line A, Line B, Lines A and B combined, Line C, Lines A–C. A six-lined verse, on the other hand, might be taught in the following sequence:

A, B, AB, CD, ABCD, EF, CDEF, Whole verse.

In doing this, the teacher can disguise the repetition in several ways, for example by varying the volume; asking groups of children to sing, rather than the whole class, asking children in a particular group (for example, the blue table or 'the robins' or those who are 4 years old, 5 years old, etc.) to sing; interspersing the repetitions with short anecdotes or discussions about the words of the song.

The pace needs to be lively, the lesson not too long and, as in any other area of the curriculum, the teacher must have high expectations of the pupils and not be content with standards which are mediocre or worse.

Improving the standard of performance

The teacher will need to give positive, supportive feedback to the children on their singing while at the same time looking for ways of improving their work. The focus might be to improve such aspects as volume, diction, stance or phrasing. Priorities will need to be established, since it would inadvisable to try to correct too many aspects in one session.

One useful technique for **improving the volume** of singing is to divide the class into small groups and to ask each group to sing on its own. When the whole class then sings together the volume will have improved, however reticent the small group singing might have been. The reason for this is unclear. It probably has something to do with the relief of singing in a large group again after being put in the more exposed position of small group work.

Too often in infant schools, children are asked to sit on the floor with their legs crossed in front of them and to sing to the teacher who is sitting on a chair or stool at a higher level. This has several disadvantages. It constricts the diaphragm and causes the children's heads to be held in an awkward position and puts strain on the throat. A better stance is achieved when children kneel to sing, since the diaphragm is not then contorted and the children can produce a more well regulated stream of air as they perform. Better still, the children could be asked to stand as they sing. This again ensures that the diaphragm is properly positioned. While standing the children should be encouraged to focus on a point on the floor about a metre in front of them. This will help them sing higher notes more easily and will avoid straining the throat.

To **improve diction**, children should be encouraged to emphasise the consonants. This can be done by asking them to lip-read messages or to send messages in this way to each other. From here they can progress to pronouncing the consonants in the words only, without making any sound in the throat. Patient repetition of a combination of such techniques over time and an insistence on high standards can have a very beneficial effect on improving children's diction. When we use our lips and emphasise consonants in formulating words, we put less strain on our vocal cords, and this helps to improve the tone.

The advice on posture will contribute to the **improvement of breathing**. Other techniques involve helping children to realise that, as they breathe, they need to fill their stomachs with air first, then their chests, and that there is no need to raise the shoulders. In breathing out the process is reversed. Asking them to breathe out onto a mirror so that it stays 'misted up' throughout the time a note is being sung will help develop control. Otherwise the child will tend to let out all the air at once and not be able to maintain a longer note. Another approach is to let the children play games such as 'Blow Football' where success relies on the ability to control the air flow while exhaling.

Improvement of pitch comes from helping children to trace the 'contour' of the melody as it is sung. One way of doing this is to ask the children to hold their hands in front of them and to raise and lower them as they sing. This process can also help **improve phrasing** and ensure that children sing right through a sentence and do not divide it arbitrarily into inappropriate chunks. Too often at the infant stage teachers fail to give the children a starting note for a song, with the result that everyone starts on a different note. While various individuals might be in tune with themselves, they are not in tune with the rest of the class, with the result that the overall effect is cacophony. It is essential therefore to give a clear starting note and to 'count the children in' while singing that note. With younger children, the vocal ranges of different children do not coincide. In these instances, it is often better to ask individuals or small groups to sing together, rather than the whole class.

Accuracy of pitching can also be helped if care is taken when choosing songs to ensure that their pitch is not too high overall. Welch (1986) for example has identified that the normal pitch for published children's songs tends to be rather too high for the natural vocal range of young children. Choksy (1974, p.17) argues that the keys of D, E♭ and E are most appropriate for pitching songs to be taught by rote. She also points to a range of research evidence which suggests that young children find descending melodic patterns easier to sing than ascending progressions and melodic leaps easier than stepwise movement.

For some children, the process of learning to pitch note accurately is particularly problematic and therefore the next section will be devoted to the issue of the 'monotone'.

HELPING THE MONOTONE CHILD

The term 'monotone' is applied to individuals who have difficulty in pitching more than one or two notes, to which they stick doggedly while others are singing the tune. The term 'growler' is also often used to describe them and this is a fairly accurate description. Occasionally, however, children will be found who do not growl at all and do not just stick to a few notes. In these cases, the children soar above everyone else, making up the most amazing elaborations while the rest of the class are singing the tune. Either way the problem is one of poor pitch singing.

It is important to be clear when poor pitch singing is a result of monotonism and when it arises from other causes. In many infant classes, out of tune singing results from the teacher's failure to give a clear starting note. In other instances, the poor pitching is a result of asking pupils with differing vocal ranges to perform together. Therefore, these possibilities have to be eliminated before it is assumed that there is a problem of monotones to be addressed.

The causes of monotonism seem to be numerous. It is amazing how often parents will make a statement to the effect that 'You can't expect Tom to sing. We're both tone deaf'. The term 'tone deaf' is too often used as post hoc rationalisation for the poor teaching that they received at school. In the same way, it is easy to blame the inability to catch a ball on 'lack of coordination' rather than on an insufficient attempt on the part of a teacher to explain that if you want to catch a ball you must keep your eye on it. It might not be possible to do anything about teaching in the past, but it is obvious that the onus is on us to ensure that we do not perpetuate the situation. Part of the process of developing effective teaching techniques is maintaining high expectations of the pupils.

In some instances, monotonism is simply a result of lack of physical development at a particular time. With increasing maturation, the child learns to control his or her vocal cords and the problem disappears.

When being taught by a man, young children often try to sing in a male voice register. Because this is too low for them, they end up growling on the lowest note that they can manage. One way of overcoming this is for a male member of staff to sing falsetto. Then the children can make a more direct comparison between their own voices and that of the teacher.

Another possible problem for young children is the pitch range of a song. If this is too high or too wide the child will not be able to sing it and, rather than trying to sing parts in tune, will resort to singing the whole song out of tune.

In some instances, it might result from lack of careful listening and focusing on the changes of pitch. It is interesting that speakers of the Korean language do not develop monotonism. This is probably because their language is pitch-orientated, so that the same word will change its meaning depending on the pitch at which it is spoken. In these circumstances the act of learning to speak demands minute attention to variations in pitch which, in turn, leads to accurate pitching in singing.

In the case of one young girl we came to the conclusion that her monotonism might well have had a psychological cause. The child was the only girl in a large family. One day her mother, the only other female in the home, deserted them. The child felt so let down by her sex that she took to dressing like her brothers, aping their mannerisms and speaking with a very low voice.

It must be emphasised that just because children cannot sing different pitches, it does not mean that they cannot hear them. In teaching sight singing and aural development to primary and secondary children, we have often found that children who are significantly worse than others in singing a range of pitches are able to identify notes played to them perfectly well. In these instances, control of the vocal mechanism seems to be lagging behind aural development.

Tackling monotonism

Just as there are many possible causes of monotonism, there are many ways of tackling it. A combination which suits one child might not suit another and there will need to be a considerable amount of trial and error. It will also take time, particularly in the most difficult cases. To add to the frustration, when a child begins to pitch correctly you can never be sure which aspect of the 'treatment' has worked. It might not even be the result of anything which you have done but merely reflect the natural maturation of the child. However, the same could be said of development in other areas of the curriculum and, however tempting it might be, this should not be used as a reason for not even attempting to tackle the issue. Probably the best approach is to give children access to a combination of approaches, although there are some basic principles that we would recommend. These are outlined below, but are not in any particular order of importance.

The **first basic principle** concerns making clear to the child what is happening. A variety of techniques can be used. Children are being taught to swim earlier and earlier and some achieve high standards at a very young age. One approach, therefore, is to ask the class how many of them can swim; how many of them can swim very well, moderately well and so on. Eventually there will be some children who will say that they cannot swim at all. Discussion of this will lead the class to realise that this is simply because they have not had a chance, not because they are incapable of doing so. In the same way there are some children who have not had as many opportunities to sing as others. Further discussion of swimming lessons will highlight the fact that novice or less experienced swimmers would not be thrown into the deep end or be expected to swim the same number of strokes, widths or lengths as other children. They would be given slightly different tasks to perform and would be given particular attention at various times. In the same way, explain that those who are less confident or experienced singers will be given special attention at various times and that the rest of the class will help them to achieve this.

Much of the special attention will consist of individual work for a very brief period during a singing lesson. For the rest of the time, the monotone children will listen while others sing. Some teachers find this difficult advice to swallow. However, if the aim is to help the child improve, that child must be given the opportunity to practise correct pitching. It is pointless giving special attention for a brief period and then letting the child sing any old note. This would simply mean that the child was spending more time practising incorrect pitches, thereby making the process of correction even more difficult; it would as absurd as spending time ensuring that children understood that $2 + 2 = 4$ and then putting them in a situation where they might say $2 + 2 = 5$ or $2 + 2 = 6$ without any correction. If the approach is unacceptable for teaching a mathematics skill, it should be equally unacceptable in the teaching of music. This approach will also ensure that children receive timely feedback, an important element in developing accurate pitch, as the research of Graham Welch (1985a, 1985b, 1986) has indicated.

A **second** and very important **principle**, which we discovered by trial and error but which is supported in research findings by Cleall (1968), is to ensure that whatever music an individual sings is within their own natural range. Most adults' and children's speaking voices tend to revolve around a particular range of notes. You can find roughly what this range is for particular children by asking them to speak. As each child does so, play around on the piano until you find a note that seems to accord with the speaker's voice. Play the note which seems to appear most often and tell the child that if he or she can speak that note, he or she must be able to sing it. Then ask the child to try to sing the note with you and to 'hold it on' for a while. It might take time for the note to develop and there will be a need to repeat the activity regularly. However, there have been cases where this simple approach has led to dramatic results.

A **third principle** is to ensure that the monotone child is placed in a position where he can listen to the pitches being sung correctly. This is best done by surrounding the monotone with good singers. As the latter perform, the monotone should be asked to listen with his or her eyes shut, to focus on how the sounds go up and down and to imagine singing the notes along with the others. We have known two cases where monotonism was cured by this method alone, but, in both cases, the rest of the class were unusually good singers and a considerable amount of time was spent on music each week in the school concerned.

A **fourth principle** is to ensure that the child can hear what s/he is singing. Very often, when they sing with others, monotone children do not seem to realise that they are not singing the same notes as the rest. It is as if they hear the overall sounds without the blemishes that they create. The same is true even of competent singers. It is difficult sometimes to know whether one is in tune with others. Folk singers usually try to overcome the problem by pressing a finger over one ear. This enables them to hear their own voices more clearly while at the same time hearing their fellow performers. The same technique can be adapted to helping children. Ask all the children, but particularly the monotones, to press their ears gently as they sing. As they hear their own voices in sharper relief, they are in a position to be able to adjust it so that it is more clearly in tune.

A **fifth principle** is to ensure that children know what is involved in singing a note. Some do not realise that more effort and tightening of the vocal cords is required when singing than when speaking. One way of demonstrating this is to allow a child to put a hand on the teacher's throat and to feel the difference in the amount of vibration and tautening of the vocal cords when sung and spoken sounds are produced. Because of their larger Adam's apples and the deeper sounds which they produce, it is easier for men to demonstrate this than for women to do so. Many children have been helped to 'put more effort' into producing a singing sound by doing this. In the following example, several of these principles are seen in operation.

A 7-year-old boy is standing at the front of the class with his eyes shut. The teacher sings a note which he performs falsetto and holds on for a long time. The child is asked to listen to the note several times. The teacher then sings it once more. This time, the child is asked to put his fingers on his ears and, when the teacher touches him on the shoulder to try to produce the same note with the teacher. The child does so and sings a note several tones lower. The exercise is repeated. This time the child is told that, if the note is incorrect, the teacher will touch him a second time on the shoulder. At that point he should listen again and then try a higher note. When this is done, the boy's note moves up slightly but it is still not in tune. The teacher compliments the boy on the improvement made. He now asks the child to imagine that there is hole in the middle of his forehead like that of a whale . As he sings, he should try to imagine that he is trying to force the sound up throughout the top of his head and through this hole. This helps to a certain extent. The boy's voice is still not in tune but he is developing more agility in moving it, and this is an important step in the right direction. It does not, however, follow that the next time the child will start from the point reached here or that he will make the same amount of progress. It is a long process where progress is through peaks and troughs, advances and reversals, rather than through straightforward and constant linear development.

Another variation on the 'hole in the forehead' is to ask a child to make a yawning sound which reaches to the highest note that he can produce. When he can do this fairly well, he should be asked to stand with his feet apart. As the pitch of his sound moves up, he should lean down and pick up an object like a lego construction from behind his feet. Repeated practice in doing this will help send the voice upwards and help develop a 'head register'.

When the voice has begun to move from one or two notes, a child can be helped to identify the sounds which he can sing by hearing them played on the chimebars. Not only does this enable the child to match sounds, it also gives him a sense of improvement and achievement. At this stage, the child can also be asked to sing simple tunes within his own pitch range.

Throughout all this type of work, the children should be encouraged to sing confidently but not too loudly. Loud singing often makes it difficult for children to relate the sounds which they are producing to the rest of the group or to the piano or other accompaniment. It is also important to ensure that, as songs are taught, they are sung slowly enough for children to have time to grasp not only the words but also the shape of the melodic line.

There is a remarkable amount of singing taking place in schools all over the country every day. Too often, however, it is treated as something incidental to the main purpose of education, rather like the colouring and drawing of pictures when a piece of written work has been completed. If schools are to help their children develop their voices to their full effect, then singing should be approached carefully, systematically and in a planned way. It is too important an activity to be treated otherwise.

Chapter 5

Instrumental performance

THE NEED TO GIVE CHILDREN ACCESS TO A WIDE RANGE OF INSTRUMENTS

Research by Moog (1976) and others suggests that very young children first react to the quality and timbre of sounds. In teaching, it is therefore very important to build on this and give them access to as wide a range of sound sources as possible. As well as the voice, these should include pitched as well as unpitched instruments, chromatic as well as diatonic instruments and also electronic and computerised sound sources. The pitched instruments should cover the full range of registers and include both wooden and metal instruments. Too often infant children are restricted to soprano chimebars and glockenspiels and denied access to instruments like the bass xylophone. Not only do these provide the pleasure of deep, rich sounds, they are also invaluable for children who suffer hearing loss, since their vibrations can be felt and heard more easily than those of higher instruments.

Another important consideration when building up a stock of instruments is to ensure that they are well made. Cheap, gaudily painted plastic instruments might be appealing to the eye and to the pocket but their life span is often very limited and therefore they are a false economy. Too often there has also been a lack of precision in the manufacture of these instruments. A xylophone, for example, might have notes which become progressively shorter but, unless the physical volume of successive bars has also been reduced to a precise degree, the notes will not be pitched correctly. In the worst instances, notes go down in pitch when they should be rising, leaving young children with a false impression of how a xylophone functions and preventing them from building up appropriate expectations about the behaviour of instruments and notes of varying lengths. This obviously detracts from any attempt to lay a firm foundation for their future musical development.

THE SOUND TABLE: ADVANTAGES AND DISADVANTAGES

Many nursery and infant schools have a sound table or sound corner, either within classrooms or in a corridor or the school hall. Several books give helpful advice on how to create such a resource (for example, Wakeley 1984, Gilbert 1981). There are several advantages to such an arrangement, not least being the opportunities that it creates for children to explore instruments for themselves, to experiment with them and to hear and feel the effects which they create.

If they are to be successful, sound corner activities should be clearly integrated into the planning for music, be closely related to activities pursued in more formal activities and be a means of reinforcing the concepts explored in those contexts. Like the school fish tank, it should be changed regularly. Too often sound tables become fixtures whose original function has long been forgotten. In one school, the sound table had become so overlaid with other detritus of classroom life that the process of finding it became almost an archaeological dig.

A sound table or corner should be accessible, safe, attractively presented and clearly labelled. It should also include a range of good quality equipment. Too often it becomes the place to park the oldest and least attractive instruments available in the school: cymbals that would have had more fulfilling existences as ashtrays, for example. The argument occasionally presented in defence of this is that it prevents the best instruments from being broken. However, children usually show considerable interest in what is new, attractive and feels and smells good. When faced with inferior equipment, their curiosity is blunted.

Sound tables are also often the receptacles for found objects or for home-made instruments. There is certainly a place for these, particularly when exploring the sounds made by everyday objects or discussing the basic principles on which instruments work. However, if the sole fare consists of squeezy bottles masquerading as maracas, paper tissue boxes bound round with elastic bands hoping to be mistaken for a guitar, cardboard tambourines with milk bottle top jingles, it will limit rather than extend children's musical experiences. Too often such home-made instruments are used as an excuse for not investing sufficiently in a wide range of real instruments. Consider the messages we are giving children about the importance of music if at one end of the classroom they see a disparate collection of home-made, badly produced and unattractively presented conglomeration of ersatz 'instruments', while at the other they find a gleaming computer.

SEQUENCE OF ACTIVITIES TO SUPPORT THE DEVELOPMENT OF INSTRUMENTAL PERFORMANCE

As has already been stressed, it is very important to give young children opportunities to experiment and play with instruments on their own.

However, the process of 'discovery' learning, as Dearden (1976) has indicated, can be helped and made more efficient by careful guidance from the teacher, particularly where children need to learn the conventions of a subject.

Classification of instruments

One such convention concerns the way that we classify instruments. They can be classified according to the way that they are made (wood, skin, brass, strings, etc.); the way they are played (for example, hit, scraped, plucked, blown, bowed); and the way they sound (clashing, rattling, jingling, and so on).

One way of helping children classify instruments is to adapt the type of activity that is often used in mathematics to help them build up sets. The teacher arranges two hoops on the floor. Into one hoop will go the instruments that are made of wood, and into the other will go those that are not made of wood. The teacher and the children discuss each instrument and decide where it ought to be placed.

The set of instruments that are not made of wood can then be further subdivided into 'skin instruments', 'string instruments', etc. and be put into further hoops. This activity can then be reinforced by asking the children to repeat the activity for themselves in relation to groups of instruments on the sound table. They could also be asked to use the same coloured crayons to colour pictures of instruments that belong to the same category and to use a different colour for instruments that belong to a different set.

Another form of reinforcement is to arrange the children in a circle, give each child a different instrument and then ask them to play it when a card with an instrument of the same type is held up. Pictures of instruments could also be collected and arranged into displays as a further support to learning.

Of course, the above reinforcement activities are equally relevant whether the focus is the material from which instruments are made or the way that they sound or are played. Combinations of classes could also be created at later stages, for example, arranging sets of wooden instruments which are struck and wooden instruments which are scraped.

Another musical convention that cannot be 'discovered' is the naming of instruments. Too often, teachers who lack confidence or musical knowledge and experience avoid teaching children the correct terms for instruments. One teacher recently argued that this was unnecessary, irrelevant and confusing for the children. Ironically, she had taught the children to apply the correct terminology very effectively in differentiating between a diplodocus, a pterodactyl and a tyrannosaurus rex. Given the fact that learning long words did not present a problem and the added fact that – even in the next millennium with its anticipated advances in genetic engineering – children are more likely to meet a tambourine than a dinosaur, this teacher's viewpoint seemed questionable, to say the least.

Identifying instruments from their sound

Despite the arguments just presented, there is little point in teaching children the names of instruments if they cannot identify their sounds. Therefore, at the very earliest stages the focus should be on the sound. The teacher might, for example, introduce the children to two very different instruments, such as maracas and a drum. He might talk to the children about the instruments, give them opportunities to make sounds on them, and also give each instrument a name. The teacher could then play a sound clue game with them. He asks a child to sit on the floor with his back to him and, on the floor in front of the child, he puts a pair of maracas and a drum. He also has examples of the same instruments on his lap. He chooses one of the instruments and asks the child to listen carefully and then to choose the instrument which corresponds with the one that he is playing. As the game is repeated over a period of time, the teacher introduces new instruments and places increasing emphasis on ensuring that the children attach the correct name to the instruments. The activity can also be made more demanding by using a larger number of instruments or by choosing pairs of instruments which are not dissimilar in the sounds that they produce. Within each class, the level of complexity can also be adapted to the varying abilities of the children concerned, so that the activities are appropriately differentiated.

Another variation of this activity involves larger numbers of children. Two lines of children sit with their backs to each other. In front of each row there is an identical set of instruments which the children have already encountered and with whose sounds they are already familiar. At a signal from the teacher, the first child in the first row chooses one of the instruments and plays it. That child's counterpart in the second line then has to select the same instrument and echo the sound just produced. The game continues in this way until the row with the highest number of correct answers wins. To reinforce the naming of the instruments, the child selecting the answering instrument is asked to name the instrument as well as to play it.

This game can be made more complicated: by increasing the number of instruments involved; by involving two instruments simultaneously; or by asking the children in the answering group to reproduce the precise rhythm played by the first group on their selected instruments.

As the children become more familiar with instruments, they can be further helped to identify their names, and match instruments and names to the sounds by playing 'snap' and sound lotto games. The children are given random sets of cards with pictures of instruments. In pairs, they play a snap game based on identical pairs of pictures of instruments. The child with the highest number of cards wins. From here, the children can progress to combinations of pictures and words. This time a picture has to correspond to its written name before 'Snap!' can be called. Children soon learn to identify the written names of instruments using this technique.

In Sound Lotto the children are given an equal number of randomly selected cards each. The teacher plays a sequence of sounds on instruments. If the instrument corresponds with the picture or word on a card in front of a child, the child discards that card. The first child to dispose of all the cards wins. As a follow up to this activity, a tape of sounds could be prepared which pairs of children could then listen to at the sound table.

Another way to help children develop familiarity with the sounds and names of instruments is to play a version of 'Pass the Parcel'. This can be made as simple or as complicated as necessary, to match the abilities, existing knowledge and experiences of the children concerned. The teacher takes two instruments, discusses and plays these with the children and then places them in the box. The children sit in a circle and sing a familiar song. As they do so, they pass the box round. When the music stops, the child holding the box reaches inside and makes a sound on one or other of the instruments, then chooses another child who has to identify which of the instruments is being played. With more able or more experienced children the number of instruments can be increased. As the children's familiarity with instruments increases, the teacher might select instruments and not tell the children precisely what is in the box. In this way, their powers of identification and naming are taxed further.

Another way of helping young children identify and respond to instrumental sounds is to play a version of 'Simon Says', where the children only respond to an instruction when the spoken command is accompanied by a sound on a given instrument. This can be made increasingly complicated by allowing the children to respond only to a specific rhythmic pattern on the given instrument. A further development would be to use several instruments, only one of which is a signal for responding to the spoken command.

Another game involves giving several children a different instrument each. Another child then sits blindfolded in the middle of the circle and has to identify which child is behind him or her from the sound of the instrument played. This can be made more complicated by involving several sounds simultaneously. With very experienced or able pupils, the game could be adapted so that all the instruments except one are played. The blindfolded child has to listen very carefully and identify which sound is missing. Very rarely, however, have we found that infant children can play this last game with any degree of success.

Exploring dynamic range

As well as identifying the sounds and names of instruments, children also need to be given opportunities to explore the range of dynamics that instruments can produce. The games already described can be adapted so that, as well as selecting instruments to match sounds already played, the children will be required to reproduce loud or soft sounds on those instruments. This could then be developed further by asking the children to make sounds in response to written indications, for example, **f** or **forte** for **loud**, and **p** or **piano** for **soft**. So that children have the experience to convert sounds into signs, as well as signs into sounds, the teacher could play sounds at a particular volume and ask the children to select the appropriate card to indicate the volume. This activity can be made more complex or simple to match the range of abilities within a particular group or to ensure that, as the game is revisited, increasing demands are made on the children and that progress is made.

Exploring timbre possibilities

In addition to responding to sounds of instruments, children also need to develop facility in performing on them. One way of doing this is to pass one instrument around a circle of children and ask each child to produce a different sound from the last child. This can be repeated with various instruments over a period of time. The class could build up a list of the repertoire of sounds that they have produced and how each sound was made. This could be allied to variations of the listening games already described by asking children to identify not only which instruments are being played but also how the sound on each instrument was produced. These activities can again be supplemented and reinforced through individual sound corner activities, using pictures and tape recordings.

Controlling instruments

From here, the children could be given experience of controlling instrumental sounds. The class sits in a circle, each child with an instrument. These instruments should be arranged so that children adjacent to each other do not have identical instruments. Starting from one point and moving around the circle, each child produces one sound. When this has been done, the children are asked to reflect on whether they actually did produce only one sound or whether some produced more than one. This will lead to discussions about the difficulty of producing one sound on instruments such as maracas or bells, where the sound depends on a rapid sequence of movements. The game can then be repeated, with the children making greater efforts to produce one sound. This usually leads to far greater concentration and improved control. From here, the teacher can move to asking the children to listen very carefully to the sound of the person playing before them. They must not play until the very last vibration of the previous sound has died away. Some sounds, such as that produced by a struck suspended cymbal, will take far longer to fade than others. This will lead to discussion of long and short sounds. The game can now be repeated with children playing the opposite of the sound they produced last time. A child who previously played a short sound will now play a long sound and vice versa. By taking different starting points and moving around the circle in different directions, a very different improvisation will emerge each time, which the children can then discuss and appraise. This process of developing instrumental control can also involve playing loud and soft sounds or combinations of sounds on loud-soft and long-short continua.

Performing accompaniments

Another technique for helping children develop facility in controlling instruments is to give the children an instrument each. At a sign from the teacher, they begin to play. As the teacher's hands rise, the sound gets louder; as they fall, the sound gets softer. From here the activity can be extended to involve signs that bring in individuals or small groups of instruments. This can then be built up into an improvisation along the lines described in the last paragraph.

As children gain greater facility in controlling instruments, they will be able to produce rhythmic patterns on them. These can be produced through echo activities, where the teacher plays a rhythmic pattern which the children then have to copy. As with many of the other activities described, the complexity of such patterns can be increased or decreased to match the differential abilities of the individual children concerned. These rhythmic patterns can then be made the basis of instrumental accompaniments.

Given that young children often find it easiest to reproduce the rhythms of words, one way of producing accompaniments is to teach the children a song and then to highlight a particular line of the music. As one half of the class sings, the other half then whispers the rhythm of the extract and claps its rhythm. Later this is transferred to an instrument to provide an ostinato accompaniment. Very interesting examples of this approach can be found in Moses (1984).

Simple drones or ostinato accompaniments can also be provided on tuned instruments. Chime bars are particularly useful for this, since the children need only be presented with the specific bars to be played. Later, the activity can be made more complicated by asking children to play specific bars from the full range of bars in a set. However young the children are when introduced to this type of activity, they should be encouraged to use two beaters and to hold them in such a way that they bounce off the note and allow it to resound. Giving children only one beater limits the sound possibilities available to them and prevents them from being able to play two note chords, for example, or moving quickly from one note to another when a simple ostinato is being played. It also sends the children up a cul-de-sac of learning, rather than equipping them with techniques which can provide a firm basis for further development at a later stage.

In providing accompaniments, it is important that instruments are used sparingly, to ensure that appropriate balance is maintained and that the instruments do not overpower the singing.

CREATING OPPORTUNITIES FOR PERFORMING TO OTHERS

As well as performing in class, children should be given opportunities to perform to others from an early age. Natural opportunities for this arise during the school year, for example at Christmas or Harvest times, or as part of an end of term concert. Careful planning should ensure that such celebrations arise from, reflect and enrich the work pursued in the classroom, and are not allowed to cut across the scheme of work. From time to time pupils should also be given opportunities to play to their peers in assemblies, for example. The success of such performances will depend very much on how much emphasis has already been placed on presentation within the classroom. However short an improvisation or a performance might be, the children must be taught to control their performances and to ensure that there is a clear 'envelope of silence' around the music which marks it out from the other sounds around it. They should also be taught to listen attentively to each other. Unless this is done, the children will be ill-prepared for listening to performances in a concert hall or other formalised venue, and we will have sold them short.

GENDER ISSUES AND VOCAL AND INSTRUMENTAL PERFORMANCE

There is considerable evidence that, traditionally, some instruments have been more closely associated with one gender than another (Neuls-Bates 1982, Bowers and Tick 1986, Pugh 1991). Thus the violin and harp, for example, are seen as more appropriate for women, and percussion and brass instruments as more appropriate for men. A fewer number of instruments are seen as appropriate for girls than those regarded as suitable for boys. This has obvious disadvantages in terms of equal opportunities for women. There is some evidence (Abeles and Porter 1978) that suggests that gender-stereotyping can begin as early as the age of three, with young children seeing the drum as being a boy's instrument and the triangle as being appropriate for girls.

It is important, therefore, that all children should have access to the full range of instruments and that the teacher monitors this – to ensure that traditional stereotypes are not being perpetuated. This also needs to be supported with illustrations of men and women playing the full range of instruments and also by ensuring that the teacher uses the feminine pronoun as well as the male pronoun to refer to conductors and composers.

Another aspect of ensuring equality of access is to ensure that boys are encouraged to sing as much as girls. Too often, singing has been seen as a feminine activity and boys are being excused at earlier and earlier ages from making an effort to sing, on the basis of some amateur psychological viewpoint which says that they feel embarrassed. Once the seed is sown, they live up to the expectation. It is important to avoid this and recognise that, at every stage, the highest standards of vocal and instrumental performance is expected of all children whatever their age, background or intellectual ability.

INTRODUCING ORCHESTRAL AND OTHER INSTRUMENTS

From their experimentation with classroom instruments, children can be introduced to orchestral instruments. One way to do so is to let them hear examples of the instruments with which they are familiar in the context of an orchestra or a band. In this way, they will be led from the known to the unknown and be helped to relate the sight of instruments to their sound. Another technique is to invite performers into the classroom to play to the children. Again, the immediacy of the experience and the sight and sound of a live performance will be far more meaningful to them than a recording or even a visit to a concert where the distance and remoteness of the players can be very confusing and off-putting for very young children.

Introducing recorders

Many infant schools try to enrich their pupils' instrumental experiences by teaching them the recorder. This has the advantage of extending the range of sounds available to the children and giving them further opportunities for instrumental performance. The disadvantages are that it can take a long time to learn the notes on the recorder and the children will tend to progress at widely varying speeds.

In view of this, we would recommend that if recorders are to be taught at infant school, tuition should be offered as an additional, extra-curricular activity, and that teachers should use appropriately-differentiated activities so that some children are able to move on while others are consolidating their grasp of the basic notes. Well-chosen music will ensure that children at these varying stages of development will still be able to play as a group.

PERIPATETIC INSTRUMENTAL INSTRUCTION

An increasing number of infant schools are now buying the services of peripatetic instrumental teachers, a service which in the past tended to be restricted to secondary and junior schools. If this type of help is bought, we would recommend that the school ensures that clear links are identified between the work pursued by the visiting teacher and that provided in the classroom, so that the two sets of experiences reinforce rather than cut across each other. Clear lines of communication also need to be established so that pupils' progress in the two situations can be monitored. We would recommend that part of the contract with the visiting teacher should include payment for regular, formalised discussions of this type. Otherwise, the experience is likely to be an unsatisfactory one for all concerned.

Another word of caution needs to be sounded in relation to the way that pupils are selected for instrumental tuition and the way that they are matched to particular instruments. Over the years, numerous tests of musical ability have been devised to try to identify which children are most likely to progress in instrumental lessons. A popular test often administered in junior schools and at the top end of some infant schools is Arnold Bentley's *Musical Ability in Children and its Measurement* (1965). This consists of a battery of tests focusing on **Pitch Discrimination**, **Tonal Memory**, **Rhythmic Memory** and **Chord Analysis**. All things being equal, the pupils whose scores fall into the top 10 per cent are most likely to make a success of learning an instrument. But all things are rarely equal, and one of the difficulties with tests of this type is that they do not take account of the attitudinal factors which can lead to a child performing far better or far worse than expected.

This was brought home to us very starkly in the case of two children: a girl who scored 100 per cent on the Bentley Test and a boy who achieved a very mediocre result. Both took instrumental lessons. The girl who, on the basis of her mark could be expected to do well, made very little progress and eventually stopped attending lessons. Discussions with her parents revealed that the mother was an opera singer who spent many hours a day removed from the family, rehearsing and practising. From a young age the girl had made it quite clear that she was tired of constantly hearing music around the house. She also appeared to be resentful of an activity which, she felt, came between herself and her mother.

In the case of the boy, there was no known history of musical performance in the family. Unlike the girl, who was vivacious, outgoing and very intelligent, he was rather introverted, isolated and not strong academically.

However, once he took up the instrument, he flourished. He was happy to spend a great deal of time alone and therefore rather relished the time spent on his own practising. As result, he made good progress. Furthermore, when his classmates heard how well he could play, they began to view him in a new light. The respect shown for his skills was a tremendous boost to his confidence and gradually he began to become more socially adept, as well as musically competent.

It might be argued that the instrument given to the girl did not suit her. This brings us to another issue surrounding the area of instrumental teaching. Ever since the 1930s, with the publication of the work of Lamp and Keys (1935), a considerable amount of research has been conducted into ways of matching pupils to instruments on the basis of such factors as personality traits, height, size of hands, shape of mouth, fullness of lips, and so on. However, the number of possible variables is so great and the pattern of interrelationship between them so complex that the evidence is largely inconclusive. These studies have also tended to mirror the lack of emphasis on the effects of attitudinal factors. Nevertheless, there are many instrumental teachers who have strongly held pet-theories about the ideal physical type for their particular instrument.

In view of all this, it is essential that any selection mechanisms – including published tests – that are applied within schools are treated with the greatest caution. There are too many parents who have been told that their children 'failed' the Bentley Test and have been discouraged from extending their children's instrumental experiences as a result.

As with many other aspects of music education, instrumental teaching has attracted a whole range of theories, some well-founded, others of which are no more than traditions handed down uncritically from one generation to the next. No theory should be taken on trust. All should be challenged and that includes those presented in this book.

Chapter 6

Composing in the infant classroom

FEAR OF COMPOSITION AMONGST TEACHERS

The popular image of a composer is of a starving social misfit, coughing up a little blood in an Austrian garret, dying young and leaving a plethora of works whose greatness remains unrecognised until he has long turned to dust in a pauper's grave. Composition is a rarefied activity for the talented, the unusual, for those apart. The thought, therefore, of being asked to conduct composition activities fills many teachers with fear because they imagine that they have to have particular skills, to have been trained in particular ways or to be in special communion with some invisible muse.

The same teachers, however, will quite happily help children to create pictures, stories, poems or plays. They are prepared to experiment and play about with materials and ideas, and are not at all discouraged by the fact that they have never exhibited a painting, published a poem or written a script. This is because they are putting their work in context. Instead of viewing their own or their children's work in art and literature against publicly acclaimed works, they see them in relation to the emerging skills of their pupils at particular points in their development. If teachers are to gain more confidence in musical composition, they must also be prepared to help their pupils experiment and play about with sounds. They should not expect their pupils to produce symphonies, although some famously talented infants have done so, but judge the end-products of their endeavours in terms of what might reasonably be expected of the children at that particular stage of development.

Until recently, that has been difficult where music is concerned. Parents and teachers are quite used to giving very young children the opportunity to paint and draw. As a result, most of us who have worked with children have some idea of what can be expected at a particular stage. We would not be surprised to find a 3-year-old drawing a house where the windows are at the corners of the building or to see a picture of a car by a 4-year-old where there are four wheels on one side. We might become rather concerned if a 7-year-old were producing a picture of a person where the arms grew directly out of the head and the hands looked like rakes. It is because of the accumulated knowledge of what might be expected of children's art work as they grow that such diagnostic tests as the 'Draw-a-Person Test' were devised to help identify normal and abnormal patterns of development in children.

In the case of music, however, the traditional lack of emphasis on composition has given us a far less clear idea of what might be reasonably expected of children at various ages or stages of development. What knowledge does exist is still far from becoming part of the day-to-day expectations of teachers and parents.

CHILDREN'S DEVELOPMENT AS COMPOSERS: SWANWICK AND TILLMAN'S RESEARCH

In recent years, however, some interesting work has been conducted in this area, particularly by Swanwick and Tillman (1986). Many of the studies of children's musical preferences and development conducted in the past tended to be devised by psychologists, and were often used for identifying musical potential and selecting children most likely to benefit from particular musical experiences, such as instrumental lessons. These tests tended to focus on small fragments of music rather than whole pieces and it could be argued that they had rather limited relevance to what went on in the ordinary classroom on a day-to-day basis.

Swanwick and Tillman adopted a rather different approach. They analysed 745 compositions, produced over a 4-year period by 48 children aged between 3 and 11 years and drawn from many different ethnic and cultural groups. The children had all received regular lessons from June Tillman, during which they had been given opportunities to make music in a variety of ways and at different levels of complexity. With the help of two independent 'judges', the compositions were analysed to try to determine whether they reflected any pattern in musical development over time. As a result, a spiral of development, which is represented in Figure 6.1, was 'discovered'.

According to Swanwick and Tillman, children progress through eight developmental modes: Sensory, Manipulative, Personal, Vernacular, Speculative, Idiomatic, Symbolic and Systematic. These stages correspond to language development (Swanwick 1991). Using Swanwick and Tillman's descriptions and the interpretations in Mills (1991) and Durrant and Welch (1995), the characteristics of children's music as they progress through the eight modes may be summarised as follows.

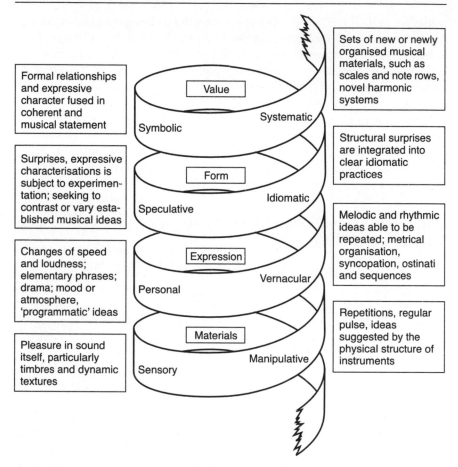

Figure 6.1 Short-hand version of the Swanwick–Tillman model
Source: Swanwick 1994, p.90

Materials

Level 1 – Sensory

At this level, children explore and experiment with instruments in an apparently random way. They seem to delight in sounds for their own sake and are fascinated by tone colour and extremes of loud and soft.

Level 2 – Manipulative

Children now show greater control of instruments. They also make some attempt to organise the sounds they make. Compositions tend to be long and repetitive and the children make use of various devices – such as a glide up and down a xylophone – which have been suggested by the nature and shape of the instrument.

Expression

Level 3 – Personal expressiveness

At level 3, children show expressiveness in their songs and instrumental compositions by using changes of speed and volume. There are signs of elementary musical phrases emerging and the children may relate their music to external ideas, such as stories or pictures.

Level 4 – The vernacular

At this level, children's compositions are less exploratory in character. They tend to have more shape and coherence and to make use of repeated melodic and rhythmic patterns. Pieces may be quite short and be more conventional and derivative.

Form

Level 5 – The speculative

Here, the children go beyond using repeated ideas to experimenting with using contrasts and producing an element of surprise by, for example, giving a piece an unexpected ending. The structural devices are not always integrated into the piece.

Level 6 – The idiomatic

Children now begin to work within a particular idiom. They may, for example, emulate the style of music which they have heard or played. Devices such as contrast and variation are integrated into the pieces. There is a concern to make sure that the harmony sounds right and that the appropriate instruments are used. Compositions become longer, and children show greater control of technique, expression and structure.

Value

Level 7 – The symbolic

At the Symbolic Level, children use formal relationships and expressive character to produce coherent musical statements. There is a strong sense of personal commitment on the part of the children.

Level 8 – The systematic

By the time that they reach this level, children have developed a distinctive, personal style which draws on their explorations of a range of idioms.
This may include making use of newly-organised musical materials, such
as scales and note rows and unusual harmonic systems.

Swanwick has been at pains to discourage too rigid and mechanical an
interpretation of the model. For example, too much could be made of the
ages attached to the layers of development. Although music development
may follow a particular sequence, it is unlikely to follow a 'standard
timetable' for all. The amount of musical stimulation in an individual's
environment might well speed up or slow down development and, therefore, there are likely to be wide variations between children at any age.

The progress throughout the layers reflects the dynamic interplay
between 'assimilation' and 'accommodation' which Piaget identified as
being central to learning. 'Assimilation' is the process of relating new experiences to our existing view of the world. But, as the new information is
processed, our view of the world alters in order to 'accommodate' it. This
interplay between assimilation and accommodation is continuous and can
involve the revisiting of earlier layers in the model. Thus, for example,
when faced with an unfamiliar style of music, we might need to focus first
on the sounds themselves (Level 1) before beginning to perceive shapes
(Turn 2) and then getting to grips sufficiently with the style to be able to
identify its expected and unexpected aspects (Swanwick 1988). It is important, therefore, to recognise that one layer is not be viewed as better or
worse than another. Each layer includes previous ones, and previous layers
may be revisited on occasion.

Swanwick and Tillman do not claim to have discovered *the* definitive
spiral of musical development. However, with the provisos outlined
above, it is a useful way of describing the development in children's
music, not only in the area of composition but also in terms of how they
use, hear and appraise musical material. Durrant and Welch (1995) have
argued that it could also be used in challenging and motivating children.
Another advantage is that it enables us to identify incongruities in our
approach to music education. For example, Swanwick (1994) describes
how, during the 1970s, many class teachers focused on the source of musical sounds in fostering 'self-expression', placing particular emphasis on
the more 'intuitive' left side of the spiral, at the expense of the more 'analytical' right side. At the same time, and often within the same institution,
instrumental teachers were emphasising the right hand side of the model
at the expense of the left. This tension is still there in many schools,
though possibly not to the same extent as in the 1970s. The important
point is to ensure that pupils are given experiences of both sides of the
spiral, so that the analytical and the intuitive are interrelated. The model

helps us to analyse our practice and identify the extent to which this is being achieved.

The approach adopted by Swanwick and Tillman has not been acceptable to everyone. Hargreaves (1986), for example, is sceptical of attempts to outline specific stages in the creative process. Mills (1991) has also warned of the dangers of generalising too much from the Swanwick-Tillman spiral, since there is a need for more evidence of its validity and reliability. A pattern that emerges in the compositions of groups of pupils, all taught by the same teacher, presumably in accordance with a particular philosophy and methodology, will not necessarily be applicable to works produced by children taught by a variety of teachers who do not necessarily share the same approaches or viewpoints.

Some of the concerns about the validity and reliability of the spiral model have been answered, to a certain extent, by a more recent study by Swanwick (1994). This was designed to answer two questions. First, was the assessment process by which data in the original study was interpreted really adequate? Second, could these findings be repeated in another culture? The original study was replicated, this time in Cyprus, using 28 compositions chosen at random from a total of 600 produced by kindergarten, primary and secondary aged children, taught by twelve teachers in all. In this study the number of judges was increased from two to seven. The results indicated that there was a statistically significant relationship between the age of children and the placing of their compositions in relation to the spiral criteria. It was also found that the sequence of developmental levels originally mapped were reasonably accurate and had predictive power. However, although the sequential order of development in the work of Cypriot and UK children was identical, the compositions of the UK children were generally more advanced. There was also greater variance among the Cypriot children. Swanwick suggests that this could be the result of the effects of different musical environments in the schools from which the children were drawn. However, he warns against reading too much into this. The number of teachers in this study was greater than in the original research. However, a key person involved in the Cypriot study was the music inspector for the island who was a research colleague of Swanwick. This could mean that the teachers involved shared the same approaches and philosophy which equated with that used by the teacher in the original study. It is possible that such factors might have influenced the results and that the pattern of development revealed by the spiral applies only to children taught along particular lines. Comparative studies involving a variety of varying styles, philosophies and approaches would therefore be needed to determine whether the pattern of development described by Swanwick and Tillman applies generally. However, setting up such an investigation would involve additional variables which might also influence the result.

A further criticism levelled at Swanwick and Tillman is that their work emphasises the general pattern of development at the expense of the particular development of the individual. However, Swanwick (1994) has been at pains to emphasise that in mapping the developmental spiral it was certainly not their aim to 'explain away the magic of musical experience or to underplay the uniqueness of individuals'.

CHILDREN'S DEVELOPMENT AS COMPOSERS: DAVIES' RESEARCH

One of the most interesting critiques of the Swanwick-Tillman spiral has been presented by Coral Davies (1992) who argues that the sample on which the study was based appeared to be biased towards instrumental music, and that this could have influenced the results. She suggests that pupils may be further advanced in their vocal creations than in their instrumental explorations and that, more particularly, young children's vocal compositions display greater concern with structure than the Swanwick-Tillman spiral would suggest.

Davies's own work (1986; 1992) on young children's vocal compositions has focused on what is unexpected and unique in each one, rather than on common patterns or sequences of development. Her studies are a development of the work of Moog (1976), McKernon (1979), Dowling (1982;1984) and Davidson et al. (1981), all of whom examined young children's vocal compositions and found evidence to suggest that, at an early age, children are sensitive to the underlying structure of the songs which they are taught and can apply the same basic principles to songs of their own creation. Davies was also influenced by the theories of musical cognitive processes identified by Sloboda (1985) and Serafine (1988). In her 1992 study, she analysed the songs of 32 children aged between 5 and 7 in two schools over a period of 18 months to see to what extent they reflected 'musical thought processes'. She found that children of 5 and 6 can invent initial ideas and add other ideas to them. They group notes into units or phrases and convey a clear notion of beginnings and endings, suggesting that they have in mind an overall frame or pattern for a song, within which specific details are developed. This sensitivity to structure enables them to organise time past, present and future into a coherent experience – a central requirement in approaching music, which exists in time and relies for its interpretation on our being able to interrelate events in time.

In discussing Davies's work, Swanwick (1994) suggests that the apparent structure in these young children's compositions might result from the nature of the words, whose sounds, patterns and meanings encourage the production of conventional structures. He accepts that the children are able to bring some order into their perceptual process. However, when these structures are combined it is unclear whether this is the result of a deliberate process or whether it is simply the result of the children's playing about, in the way that they can play about with language and produce statements that appear to have greater depth of meaning than the children themselves actually understand. There is, therefore, a danger of reading more into the youngsters compositions than might really be there.

The debate is by no means over and the evidence is far from conclusive. However, it is clear that from a very early age young children make up their own music, and by the time they come to school they have already had considerable experience as 'composers.' The teacher's task is to capitalise on this and extend the children's experiences further, so that they have a wide range of opportunities to engage in activities that clearly have an important role to play in their development as musicians.

The remainder of this chapter will focus on some ways in which this might be done.

COMPOSITION IN PRACTICE IN THE CLASSROOM

There are several stages which are common to any classroom composition activity. These may be summarised as follows:

- exploration of sounds;
- selection of sounds;
- drafting and redrafting of ideas;
- finalising the form of the composition.

These stages are not mutually exclusive and will not necessarily be pursued strictly in this order. The process of redrafting, for example, might involve the children in searching for new sounds and therefore returning to the first stage described above. The amount of time spent on each stage, and the degree of independence exercised by the children, will depend on their age, stage of development, abilities and experiences. In general, however, the younger the children, the more help and direction they will need from the teacher.

Two other developments can also be expected during Key Stage 1. First, as the children get older they will be better able to cope with working together in pairs or groups. Second, the stimuli for composition will change in character. In the early stages, the starting point might be the production of sound effects reflecting some aspect of a child's 'concrete' experience, such as the weather, toys and so forth. By the end of the key stage, the children will be better able to respond to more abstract starting points. These developments are reflected in the following examples of composition activities being pursued by classes of different ages.

Example 1: illustrating poems using sounds

For this reception class activity, the teacher has chosen to teach the children two poems from *'The Walker Bear Children's Treasury'*. The first, 'Ten in the Bed' by Penny Dale, is a variation on the wellknown song but instead of children, a variety of cuddly toys – a hedgehog, zebra, teddy bear, elephant and so on – fall out of bed as their owner sleeps. Each animal produces a different sound as it falls: Bump!, Ouch!, Thump!, Donk! etc. The teacher has assembled ten fluffy toys to correspond to the animals in the poem and the children have learnt to sequence the animals so that they know the order in which the animals fall out. Most of the children have also learnt to associate a particular sound with each animal.

Now the teacher assembles a range of instruments and the children spend time trying out the sounds on the instruments and getting used to them. She then asks the children which instrumental sounds they think best fit the sounds made by the animals as they fall out of bed. There is a considerable amount of discussion as the children decide whether a drum is better for the 'Bump!' of the hedgehog or for the 'Thud' of the crocodile. Eventually, a specific instrument is assigned to each of the animals. This activity extends over several short sessions, spread across the week.

Once instruments have been matched to animals, the children practise performing the poem, with individual children playing their instruments on the appropriate cue. From time to time, as they perform, the children discover slightly different ways of producing a sound on their particular instruments. The teacher draws attention to this when it happens and discusses with the class which sound they think is best. In this way, the children are involved in each of the four stages of exploration and selection of sounds, drafting and redrafting of ideas, and presenting a final version of their composition.

Example 2: using body sounds to produce a rain piece

The topic for the half-term for this Y1 class is weather and the teacher has used this as a starting point for work in several areas of the curriculum, including music.

Exploration of sounds: whole class work followed by smaller group work.

The children sit in a circle with the teacher and play an imitation game. She tells them that when she makes a gesture, they must copy her. If she claps her hands, they must clap back. If she stamps her foot, they must stamp back and so on.

When the children have had some practice in doing this, the teacher asks them to listen to how loudly she is making her sounds and to reflect that in the sounds that they produce. The success of this varies. Some children make some attempt to reflect the volume as well as the gesture. Others are still having some difficulty in reflecting the gesture.

From here, the teacher progresses to asking individual children to take the lead in the activity and to decide on the sounds to be imitated. This work is followed up by a parent helper who, at the end of morning or afternoon sessions, asks various groups who have completed their other work to play the imitation game with her. This proves to be particularly useful in giving the class a constructive activity to pursue while waiting for some of the slower ones to get changed ready for PE.

Exploring sounds further: whole class and group work

The session starts with a replay of the imitation game, this time with the teacher being more insistent on the accuracy of imitation, both in terms of the nature of the gestures and their volume.

The children now sing a song about the sounds they can make with their hands and feet and make gestures and sounds of their own as they perform it. The teacher then takes a series of cards on which there are pictures of hands clapping, feet stamping, etc. She now leads the children in the imitation game, this time using the picture cues. When they have grasped how to do this, individual children volunteer to hold up the cards.

This develops into a simple notation exercise, where the teacher or one of the children, arranges the pictures in a particular sequence and the children then have to play their sounds in the correct order.

Selection of sounds

In this session, the teacher plays and discusses a recording of weather sounds. The children are asked to identify sounds of heavy rain, individual rain drops, thunder, etc. and to match these to the relevant pictures.

The teacher now asks the children what happens when the weather changes from a sunny to a stormy day. As a result of the discussion, they arrange the picture cards into a sequence. Card 1 shows a sunny day; in Card 2, a few rain drops appear; in the next card the rain is very heavy; this is followed by a picture of lightning, and so on. The final sequence of cards is put onto a large display board.

The next session starts with a recap of the sound-copying games played earlier. The teacher then goes on to explain that they are now going to use the hand and feet sounds with which they have been experimenting to make sounds to match the pictures on the display boards. The children look at the first picture. One child decides that there should be no sound for this picture at all. The teacher challenges him and asks the class to think of a recent warm day. What types of sounds did they hear? They recall sounds of birds and children playing. Then she asks them whether there was any wind. They cannot recall any but the teacher reminds them of the slight breeze that they had felt at the time. How could they make that sound? Some children start to make whistling noises. The teacher reminds them that they are only to use hands and feet sounds and asks, Could they use their hands to produce a sound? She prompts them by reminding them of the sound produced when they had all rubbed their hands together. They try this out.

Drafting and redrafting

The next stage is to ask whether the sound will be at the same volume all the while. No, they decide, it will get louder and softer. The class then experiments with ways of doing this and thereby starts on the process of drafting and redrafting the piece. This is done for each of the pictures until a final piece is reached. At each stage, the children are encouraged to comment on the sounds produced and to explore further possibilities. Thus, they are involved in listening and appraising activities, as well as performing and composing.

The final form

The class now performs the whole piece (finalising the form of the composition). Some children forget what they are suppose to do and the performance breaks down. After a few attempts, however, the teacher announces that the piece is now ready to be recorded. Two children who are the 'recording engineers' for the week take responsibility for setting up the tape recorder and microphone, loading the tape and giving the cue to start and stop performing.

Later the tape-recording will be made available in the listening corner as part of the display work that the class is building up on the Weather Project. The teacher will also use it as a basis for further discussion of the piece, to help the children remember how various effects were produced, and possibly to prompt them into thinking how the piece might be improved if they were to work on it again.

You will notice that when the children are selecting sounds they are made to choose body sounds and not to include whistling and other new sounds. This might appear too limiting at first. However, if children are not given a specific focus, they will be unlikely to explore the possibilities in the sounds available to them. Part of the process of being a creative artist is to have to work within constraints. Children who are asked to write haiku, where the number of syllables in each of the three lines is strictly defined, often produce far more concentrated and vivid poems in the long run than if they are given too free a hand. Professional composers have to produce music for realistic and available resources if they ever hope it to be performed. This is illustrated in the case of Stravinsky and Messiaen. In the early part of his career, Stravinsky wrote extended works for very large and lavish orchestral resources. However, with the outbreak of the First World War, many of these orchestras became depleted and the venues for performances became limited. The composer adapted to this by creating works which could be performed by a small number of performers in limited spaces with the minimum number of props. Messiaen wrote his *Quartet for the End of Time* for a motley group of professional musicians who were incarcerated with him in a prisoner-of-war camp. He worked within the constraint of the musical resources available to him, as well as the other constraints and tyrannies of prison life, to produce what is undoubtedly one of the most remarkable chamber works of this century. Therefore, the insistence on working within defined limits gives the children an early experience of the discipline required by composition.

Example 3: telling a story through pictures, movement and music

A class of mixed aged YR and Y1 children has been singing 'Hickory Dickory Dock' to a simple accompaniment: a child has maintained the beat, using a woodblock, while a simple two-note ostinato has been played by the teacher.

The class is now presented with pictures of the events in the story: the mouse coming into the room; the mouse climbing up the clock, the clock striking 'one' and the mouse scurrying away. The teacher shows the first picture to the children and asks them to tell her what is happening. She then asks John to go to the door of the classroom and to pretend to be the mouse coming in, seeing the clock and moving towards it. Before he does so, she asks the class to suggest ways that he will move. Will he move quickly or slowly? The class decides that he should move slowly. John tries this and walks across the room slowly. When she sees this performance, Sarah suggests that John should run in because that's how a mouse moves. She demonstrates. The teacher then asks them whether a mouse would run straight in as Sarah has done. After some discussion, Laura suggests that the mouse could come slowly to begin with and then run. The teacher refines this by suggesting that, in addition, the mouse might stop at intervals to look round before moving on. Edward decides that he could demonstrate this and does so fairly successfully.

The teacher now draws the children's attention to a collection of pitched and unpitched instruments that she has assembled. These include a suspended cymbal, a guiro, a tambour, a pair of maracas, a wooden agogo and a glockenspiel. The children have already encountered these instruments before but a few minutes are spent reminding the children of the name of each instrument and the sound which it makes.

Edward is asked to repeat the mime that he performed earlier. The children are then asked to suggest the best sound for signalling the entry of the mouse into the room. One child suggests that the tambour would be best. Another suggests the maracas. A third suggests that the guiro would be most effective. As each suggestion is made, the child who made it is invited to make his or her sound as Edward moves. The class watches, listens and then discusses the effect. Eventually the children opt for the guiro.

The teacher then asks how the mouse knows that there is a clock in the room. Some children answer: 'he can see it'. After further prompting and questioning, someone suggests that the mouse can also hear the clock. The next step is to find a sound to represent the clock. It does not take long before most of the children decide that the wooden agogo would be best.

The agogo sound is now added to Edward's mime. In an attempt to refine it further, the teacher asks the class: 'what happens if you move nearer the clock?'. This causes considerable confusion. To try to overcome this, the teacher plays a tambourine fairly softly and, starting from one end of the room, moves towards the children. Some can tell that the tambourine gets louder with the approach of the teacher. But when the teacher re-presents the question 'what happens if you move nearer the clock?', the children cannot answer. Eventually, she stands at one end of the room playing the agogo and the children move towards her. They now realise that the sound gets louder. Whether the confusion has been caused by the change of instrument from the agogo or by the teacher's moving towards the class, rather than the other way round, is unclear. Now, however, the class is in a position to add the sounds of the agogo to the original sounds and the mime.

During this session, the children have been involved in each of the activities of: **exploring sounds, selecting sounds and drafting and re-drafting ideas**. The final form, however, will not take place until the next session.

The second session begins with a recap of the activity from the earlier lesson. This time, the discussion is extended to the second picture, where the mouse runs up the clock. The same sequence is used as before. The children discuss the picture, experiment with movements, explore sounds and match them to the mime. For this second scene, different children take the roles of instrumentalists and mime artists. The xylophone has been added to the collection of instruments and the children decide to play an upward glissando on it, to represent the mouse running up the clock. In the third session, this is modified, after discussion, to a series of step-wise movements, rising in pitch followed by a downward glissando, as the mouse scurries away. The clock striking 'one' is represented by a loud cymbal clash.

From here the children progress to putting the whole composition together and performing it live to another class which they have invited to watch and hear them.

Example 4: loud and soft sounds

In previous lessons, the children in a Y2 class have been concentrating on loud and soft sounds. They have done this by singing a specially composed song which emphasises dynamic contrasts. They have listened to sounds around them, made pictures of the sound sources and grouped them under the headings 'loud' and 'soft'. They have also played a version of the 'Simon Says' game, where they are allowed to respond to a spoken instruction only if it is accompanied by a drum-sound played at a particular volume. In addition, they have listened to recordings of loud and soft music.

Session 1 Now the children are sitting in a circle, each with an instrument. The teacher is sitting with the children. She explains that when she points to a particular child, that child should begin playing and continue to do so until she makes a different gesture to indicate 'stop'.

The class practises this for a few moments. The teacher now explains that when she raises her hand high in the air the performers should play a loud sound, and when she lowers her hand the sound should be soft. The children experiment with this for a few minutes.

Now that the class understands what has to be done, the teacher invites a child to take her place as the conductor. The game is played as indicated. At first, the conductor tends to move too quickly between the extremes of sound and does not give clear instructions of when to start and stop. However, this problem is ironed out and various conductors take turn in leading the group. Some children also have difficulty in finding ways of making soft or loud sounds on their instruments. But, after experimenting with the sound, this situation is improved to a certain extent.

In this first session the emphasis is on exploration of sounds.

Session 2 This session starts with a recap of the previous activity. Then the teacher explains that the conductor should not simply start and stop performers willy nilly. Instead, some attention should be given to the particular combinations of sounds heard and to the different impact of the loud and soft sounds. There is therefore a move towards the **selection of sounds**.

When a particular improvisation has been performed, the teacher asks the class to describe what happened. From here, she prompts them to think what changes could be made. As children make their suggestions, they are invited to assume the role of the conductor. Then the new version is discussed and further changes are made. This constitutes the **drafting and redrafting stage**.

The original intention was that the **final form** would be performed twice but there is insufficient time for this, although the last improvisation of the afternoon is played twice and there is some semblance of a final version.

Example 5: timbre and form

Later in the year, the same class is involved in a more complex activity, focusing on 'timbre' and 'form'. This is pursued over several sessions.

Session 1 This lesson is held in the school hall. The teacher has brought together a range of untuned instruments. She starts by discussing the instruments and asks the children to identify which ones are made of wood, skin and metal. These are then arranged into three groups, in three widely separated areas of the hall. The children are assigned to a group and instrument. Each group is given a leader. The teacher reminds the class of the improvisation work described earlier in Example 4. Each group then improvises along the lines described there. During this, the children move through each of the stages of **exploration, selection, drafting, redrafting.**

Now each group is asked to perform its **final form** to the rest of the class. From here the teacher progresses to asking the children how the three sets of improvisations could be brought together. The first version has the metal instruments starting, followed by the skin and then the wooden instruments. After discussion, a different sequence is tried where each group plays in turn. Then one child suggests that 'everybody could play at the end'. This is tried and meets a fair degree of approval from the class.

Session 2 This starts with a repeat of the activities from the first session. This time, however, the teacher guides the class round to the realisation that it would be possible to bring one group back. After much experimentation, discussion, drafting and redrafting, the following sequence is produced:

metal–wood–skin–metal–wood–skin–everybody.

This is recorded on tape.

Session 3 This starts with the playing of the recording of the improvisation from the previous session.

This time the teacher presents the children with several large card shapes: circles, squares, triangles. She explains that a circle represents metal instruments, a triangle represents wooden instruments and that a square denotes skin instruments. After some discussion, the children are able to 'notate' the overall shape of the piece to which they have listened so that, on the hall floor, the shapes are arranged as follows.

circle–triangle–square–circle–triangle–square–a star shape, which the children have decided should be cut out specially to represent all the performers playing together.

Session 4 In this session, the children are asked to take the card shapes, decide which shape represents which groups of instruments, and then arrange a pattern that the class subsequently performs. Different patterns are tried out and the children reflect on them and refine them until they arrive at the final version. They make a recording of this and also draw the sequence of shapes which they can then display in the listening area as a 'score' of their improvisation.

There are many further ideas which could be included to illustrate development and progression in children's composition work. However, we hope that the examples outlined here will at least demonstrate that composition is a very practical, down-to-earth activity, far removed from the rarified atmosphere in which people often imagine it taking place.

Chapter 7

Listening and appraising

GENERAL LISTENING SKILLS

Listening is clearly a very important aspect of the education of the young child. The National Curriculum Programme of Study for English requires teachers to encourage their pupils 'to listen with growing attention and concentration' and 'to respond appropriately and effectively to what they have heard'. As we saw in Chapter 1, music has a very important contribution to make to the development of such skills. We should not, however, confuse generic skills of this type with the type of listening in which we are involved in music. Within the music curriculum, we should be focusing on the development of a particular type of listening and on using it in particular ways and for particular purposes.

Active and passive listening

We can use music in a variety of ways: as a relaxant at the end of a hard day at work or as background to ironing clothes, painting the kitchen, weeding the garden, wining and dining or other more exotic activities. But when we are using music in this way, we are more likely to be hearing it, rather than listening to it. It is the equivalent of being aware of pictures on a wall or of an attractive country scene, without attending in any detail to the interplay of light and shade or the juxtaposition of colours in those pictures or scenes.

The listening in which we are involved as musicians is a very different type of activity. In his Charles Eliot Norton lecture (1952) Aaron Copland describes this as 'talented listening' involving 'first, the ability to open oneself up to musical experience; and second the ability to evaluate critically that experience'. This echoes the sentiments of Stravinsky in his earlier lecture (1947) within the same series. The violinist tuning an instrument, the tenor listening to the tone that he is producing and trying to balance it with other voices in the choir, the composer selecting and rejecting specific sound combinations are all involved in an active critical process. They are not in a passive state where sounds simply wash over them. Active listening can also be developed when we attend to live or recorded performances, either alone or as part of an audience.

To emphasise this, the National Curriculum (England) does not simply refer to listening but to 'Listening and Appraising'. The National Curriculum (Wales) uses only the word 'Appraising'. Appraising involves responding to music at an intellectual as well as an emotional level (Pugh 1980). Traditionally there has been a popular tendency to divorce these two aspects of our make-up but, as Hirst and Peters (1970) have pointed out, this is a false dichotomy. In an every day situation, before we can feel frightened we must first interpret a situation as posing a threat to our own or others' safety. At the same time, it is our emotions which direct our attention to the specifically threatening aspects of that situation. Recent studies of musical perception (Odam 1995, p85) have consistently indicated that trained musicians use the analytical left side of the brain as well as the more 'emotional' right side when listening to music. Non-musicians, on the other hand, tend to use only the emotional right side. If we are to justify the time spent listening to music in school, we must ensure that it is clearly orientated to training children to develop the listening skills of musicians, rather than the more limited skills which they might develop otherwise.

Lack of focus on active listening in schools

Discussions with teachers and headteachers of infant schools often reveal considerable confusion about what is meant by listening and appraising. Many refer to it as 'music appreciation' and even some OFSTED reports have used this terminology. This might account for the way that it is often approached in our schools. What might be described as the 'Music Appreciation Movement' enjoyed a particular influence in the first half of the twentieth century, particularly as a result of the work of Percy Scholes who recognised the potential of new broadcasting and recording technologies to bring music to a larger audience. Unlike other pioneers in the field, such as Stewart Macpherson, Scholes was less concerned with presenting analyses of pieces of music than with reaching the listener directly. In attempting to 'humanise the subject' he focused a great deal on anecdotes about composers and on the 'stories' told in music (Moutrie 1976). While this had the advantage of making music available in a palatable form to a vast number of teachers and children, it also resulted in an over-emphasis on the extraneous information about music at the expense of the direct experience of music. This legacy is still with us and is reflected in the expectation among many teachers and other adults that music should 'tell a story' or conjure up a picture in our minds, or that time in music lessons should be spent on discussing the childhoods of composers. As Salaman (1983) and Paynter (1982) have warned, this detracts from the central purpose of music education.

THE USE OF RECORDED MUSIC

Another legacy of the 'Music Appreciation Movement' is the emphasis on recorded music. It is right that we should make use of such music in schools, since most of the music that we hear comes to us on radios, personal CD and stereo systems. There are many advantages in being able to get to know music in detail by listening to it over and over again. At the same time, we must be aware of several potential pitfalls in using recorded music with young children. As Bentley (1975) stresses, recordings only convey part of the picture.

Most adults will have had some experience of live performance in one form or other. They are likely to know what various instruments and combinations of instruments look and sound like and, in listening to recordings, will be able to relate what they hear to such live experiences. Young children will have had fewer experiences of live music-making and, in many instances, they might not have had any such experiences. Therefore, it will be very difficult for them to relate a recorded sound to its live equivalent and to bring the same range of associations to the event that an adult brings.

Whether listening to live or recorded performances, children are also likely to listen in different ways from adults. Adults will probably be able to differentiate between a solo voice or instrument and its backing and be able to focus on specific rhythmic patterns or melodic patterns, if their attention is drawn to these elements. This is true even of those with limited musical experiences or interests. We must not assume that children will react in the same way. Moog's work (1976), for example suggests that young children hear music in a more holistic way than adults. Most of the 2- to 3-year-olds in his study had difficulty in identifying the melodies of songs when they were divorced from their words and played on an instrument. But even if children can differentiate between the various constituents of an experience, it does not follow that they will attend to the specific aspects on which the adult wants them to focus.

This is true of many experiences in a young child's life. A friend recently described how, as a 4-year-old in the 1950s, he was made to stand in the village square to wave a paper flag at a member of the royal family who would be passing through when visiting a nearby town. At first he had hoped to see a gold carriage with a bejewelled princess inside. He was soon disabused of this and told to look out for a lady wearing a large hat who would be waving at him as her car drove by. When the motorcade arrived, he waved his flag furiously at a smartly dressed woman in a hat who duly smiled and waved back at him. It was only later that he learnt that the princess – a famously temperamental royal – had ignored the children entirely and that the person who had smiled and waved at him was a local magistrate driving a Morris Minor. A young child, therefore, cannot be relied on to extract the salient element from a large number of stimuli. Thus, when children are told to listen to the trumpet soloist in a recording of an extract from a concerto, there is no guarantee that they are not focusing their attention on the violins or the woodwind section which might be playing at the same time.

To combat this, it is important to ensure that young children are given plenty of opportunity for live music-making and that any listening to recorded music in which they take part arises from, and is related to, those live experiences. Below are some examples of this approach in action.

Examples of listening arising from live performance

A class of 5-year-olds have been listening to the sounds around them and deciding whether they are loud or soft. They have also been practising producing loud and soft sounds on a range of instruments and have sung a lullaby, 'Rock-a-bye Baby', softly and 'The Farmer in the Dell' and 'Ring-a-Ring-o'-Roses' loudly. In order to extend these experiences, the teacher now plays them two musical extracts, the opening of Debussy's 'Syrinx' and Katachurian's 'Dance of the Gladiators' and ask the children to identify whether the music in each case is being played softly or loudly.

At a different point in the year, the same children sing and act out a song about a train which gets faster and slower. They also experiment with a metronome to identify how different settings result in its producing faster and slower ticks. From here, the children progress to listening to Handel's 'Largo' and Mussorgsky's 'Ballet of the Unhatched Chickens' and are helped to identify how the first extract is slow and the second fast.

In both of these examples, the children have been given live experiences of the relevant concepts before being asked to identify how they are applied in the music. They have a sense of purpose and listen with a fair degree of concentration because they have been given a specific element to listen for.

The same sequence – live performance followed by active, focused listening – can be applied to any of the musical elements. For example, children can be asked to listen and decide:

- whether a piece of music 'skips', 'walks' or 'gallops';
- whether a melody is high or low;
- whether the music is played smoothly or staccato;
- whether the same tune is heard more than once in the course of a piece;

- at which point a rhythmic pattern which the children have been clapping appears;
- at what point a cymbal crash, drum or other instrument that they have already encountered is heard in the music.

The music will make sense to the children because it will relate to their existing experiences. Children who have improvised a piece about a rain storm or who have made up a march are likely to listen with far greater understanding and interest to works on the same themes by established composers than if they are asked to listen to the pieces 'cold'. 'Those who have made up their own music are usually more discerning when they hear the music of others.' (DES 1985)

Musical styles and listening resources

For this approach to be successful, the school will need to build up a library of listening resources. The tapes and CDs should be chosen to reflect the musical elements in practice and should be drawn from as wide a range of styles and cultures as possible. Teachers will no doubt have their own musical preferences and the enthusiasm which they feel for a particular piece can be a great spur if transmitted to the children.

However, they should guard against over-influencing or limiting their children's preferences. If children are to be helped to develop independence of action and thought, they must be given as wide a range of experiences as possible from which they can develop their own tastes. Teachers should neither limit the range of music made available (Bentley 1975), nor should they pre-judge what type of music is suitable for children and avoid presenting them with 'difficult' music (Meyer-Denkmann 1977).

Listening to a piece only once or twice will not help children to become acquainted with it. As with stories, they need to build up familiarity by returning to the music several times, on their own as well as with others. It is therefore very important that there is not only a collection of cassettes and CDs within a school library but the facility – through listening stations, for example – for children to listen to these on their own, in pairs and in small groups, as well as in a full class. This equipment needs to be of a high standard. From a very early age, children are used to hearing music played on highly-sophisticated equipment. They are unlikely to react well to poorly-reproduced performances on inferior school equipment

CREATING OPPORTUNITIES FOR LISTENING

The examples above describe listening activities in the classroom. But further opportunities for listening can also be created as a means of consolidating and extending classroom experiences.

Listening in assembly

Many schools try to extend their pupils' listening experiences by playing music to them as they walk in to assembly. Too often, however, the opportunity is not used to its full effect. The music is used simply to calm the children down and is turned off as soon as they have all entered. In many cases, this is done very abruptly with no attempt to use any of the subtleties of fading. Playing music as children walk out of assembly has even less value as an opportunity for developing listening experiences. The notion that someone could develop an appreciation of the details of a painting by moving further and further away from it is clearly absurd, and yet it is very difficult to convince teachers of the equal absurdity of pretending that children can respond to the subtleties of music as they move further and further away from the source of the sound. The only way it might have some value would be if the school had a sophisticated piped music system which kept the volume constant.

If music is to be played as an introduction to assembly, we would suggest that the following approaches need to be adopted if it is to contribute to the development of children's listening skills. First, the children should be given time to listen to the music with concentration. This might take the form of replaying it once everybody is in the hall or even delaying playing any music until everyone is in place. Before the music is played, the children should be given a specific focus for listening. For example, they could be asked to listen to the way that a particular instrument (previously encountered live) is used in the music, or how volume changes are employed. This could be developed into a theme for the week. This could take several forms, for example,

- composer of the week: where several works by the same composer are played and a short information display is presented – possibly at the entrance to the assembly hall – giving biographical details and showing pictures of the composer;
- instrument of the week: where several pieces involving the same instrument are heard. Again, this could be backed up with a display giving relevant information about the instrument and possibly including pictures of famous performers on the instrument;
- music from a particular historical period being studied, where a range of examples of several composers' music could be heard;
- atmospheric music, where the children are given the opportunity to hear the way that a particular idea – such as a storm scene – has been explored by various composers;
- music from particular countries to tie in with work in geography;
- music to correspond with world festivals, for example, Hanukkah, Chinese New Year, Diwali, etc.

Whatever the music that is played, the children should be given the opportunity to listen to it in silence. Commentary over the music as it is played is as bad as asking children to study a painting while you jump up and down in front of it.

Adapting story time

Assemblies are not the only opportunities for extending children's listening activities. Most infant schools end the day with a story. There is no reason why this time should not be extended to other activities; many schools already use it to read poetry or to discuss a painting. On the same principle it could be used for collective listening.

Other times that could be used for listening are while the children are drinking their milk or waiting for other children to finish changing for PE. As with assembly and story time, these occasions could be used to enable the children to re-hear pieces that they have already encountered, to introduce them to new works or to make them aware of the resources which they might then choose to listen to on their own.

Listening centres in the music corner or resource base would help extend this further.

Involving children in listening to live musical performances

As well as listening to recordings, children also need to be given opportunities to hear live performances. Many such opportunities will arise naturally from within lessons when, for example, children are asked to sing or play to each other or when they listen to their classmates performing a composition that they have made. These types of activities can also be extended beyond the classroom, for example by creating opportunities in assemblies for children to listen to each other performing songs or compositions on a specific theme.

In the past, many local education authorities arranged school concerts involving visits to performances by professional artists at public concert halls. The intention was to provide opportunities, which many children might not otherwise get, to extend their awareness of what the arts had to offer and to stimulate interest, which would lead children to want to go to further concerts and thus become the concert audiences of the future. No doubt many children benefited from this and many adults ascribe their love of music to the enthusiasm kindled by such experiences. However, there were many disadvantages to such an arrangement, particularly where young children were concerned.

The experience for many was a bewildering one, where they were hustled into an extremely large hall to watch oddly dressed musicians, who appeared to be miles away, going through strange rituals in the performing of music which they had not heard before and might never hear again. The remoteness of the performers and presenters was often daunting, with the result that the only meaningful, comforting and memorable aspect of the visit was the ice-cream at the interval.

Gradually these disadvantages were recognised and the arrangement was changed so that, instead of bringing children to the musicians, the musicians came to the children. In many cases, the large-scale concert series was replaced by a school-based project. This meant that the children were on their home ground and could have the opportunity to meet the performers and work with them, so that the sense of remoteness was removed and the whole activity became more meaningful and human. The most successful ventures of this type arose from close collaboration between the local authorities, the schools and the musical companies.

With the advent of Local Management of Schools and changing emphases in the roles of their personnel, many LEAs have become less directly involved in this type of work. However, in many instances it has been taken over by the education department of opera companies and orchestras. There are also increasing numbers of freelance groups and soloists who offer such services, and schools would be well-advised to explore ways of enhancing their provision through involvement with such ventures.

If a school is going to embark on ventures of this type, it should not treat them as one-off events, divorced from the normal curriculum. Instead, they should plan the project work so that it arises from and enhances work which the children have already been pursuing. If they have been pre-pared in this way, the children are likely to benefit far more from the experience than would otherwise be the case.

Chapter 8

Music and movement

INTRODUCTION

A small child is sitting in her car seat on a long journey. 'Where is Love', from the musical *Oliver*, is being played on the cassette player. She says very little and makes very little noise, except to insist on hearing the same music for a mind-numbing nth time. Every now and again she lets out a great sigh. Then her parents notice something interesting. The sigh coincides with the end of the musical phrases. Some kind of internal activity seems to be taking place which is reflected in this physical action of sighing.

It is a hot summer's day in one of our historic cities. In the middle of the pedestrian precinct, a jazz group is busking, watched by camera-happy tourists and shoppers. The child is now 3 years old. Her mother decides that, in order to get her shopping done, it will be easier to leave her and her father to watch the musicians. Half an hour later she returns to find that there is an even larger crowd of spectators and the jazz band has now been joined by another performer – her 3-year-old. The 'performance area' has also been extended by the spectators, so that the child can make full use of the space to create her movements. At first, the child responds to the music but, as a rapport builds up between her and the buskers, they begin to respond to her movements. Eventually, she realises this and, for a short while, she changes the course of the music by changing her movements from wide sweeping gestures to small 'spiky' movements and so on. She is controlling the music through her movements.

At home, she carries on this process, insisting that her father makes up music on the piano for her to dance to. But it soon becomes evident that what she wants to do is to dictate the course of the music through her gestures. For a few weeks this becomes a much-repeated activity to be demonstrated to doting uncles, aunts and grandparents.

About seven years later, the same child is listening to the car radio. She has just heard a section of Katachurian's 'Sword Dance' and is now listening to a slow section of a Baroque oboe concerto. Suddenly, she switches it off. Why has she done that? Does she not like the music? No, she does like it but she preferred the first piece. Why was that? She doesn't know really. When pressed, she says that she liked the way the first piece went. She liked . . ., and here she pauses. She liked the . . ., and she makes a very firm, almost aggressive, wide-moving gesture with both arms outwards in an arc from her chest. But the other piece, she says, is far more . . ., and again she does not use a word but makes a slow, smooth, slightly undulating pattern with her right hand. This time the movement is also accompanied by a change of facial expression, to a rather more worried look, as opposed to the great wide-eyed stare and puffed out cheeks that accompanied the first gesture.

Here, in the case of one child, we see a clear relationship between music and gesture. This is by no means unusual and, in view of existing research findings, hardly surprising.

TRADITIONAL RELATIONSHIP BETWEEN MUSIC AND MOVEMENT

In many cultures, music and dance have traditionally been very closely related. Gwynn Williams (1971) quotes a wide variety of sources to illustrate this, particularly with relation to Celtic and other European folk music. Nketia (1986) shows that in Africa music which is integrated with dance, or which stimulates motor response, is far more common than music for contemplation. Odam (1995) also refers to such links in the dance music of India and in English morris dancing. This relationship has traditionally been felt to be particularly strong where the music of young people is concerned and there are many references to it in publications from the first half of the twentieth century. Margaret Glyn, for example, writing in 1909, claims that 'a musically gifted people will always be found to have associated dancing with music, for dancing is an even greater stimulant of rhythmic feeling than is music, especially with young people' (Gwynn Williams 1971).

This emphasis has been reflected at various times in our state education system. The Board of Education's *Handbook of Suggestions* (1937) included detailed guidance on teaching music and movement in England's elementary schools. According to Taylor (1989), the use of movement in the teaching of music was particularly popular from the time of the publication of the Cambridgeshire Report (1933) until the mid-1950s. Shiobara (1994) points to a recent revival of interest in music and movement in the Japanese education system, a revival which she argues, can also be found in this country.

In early years classrooms, there is certainly an expectation that music and movement are interrelated. Nursery and infant children are taught to sing and perform finger rhymes or to march, skip and dance 'in time to the music' or to illustrate the picture conjured up by a piece of music with 'appropriate' movements. However, British teachers who use music in this way often find it difficult to explain why they are doing so. It is almost like the last vestige of a folk memory, something which is done because it has always been done. If these types of activities are to be used to full effect and be welded into a coherent, rationally-defensible programme, it is important to articulate the underlying theory. It is to this that we shall now turn our attention.

THE IMPORTANCE ON MOVEMENT FOR LEARNING IN GENERAL

The importance placed on the interrelationship between movement and learning reflects general theories of child development. For Piaget (Beard 1969) learning at any age needs contact with concrete reality and with physical manipulations of the environment. This is particularly important at infant school level where the child is likely to be at what Piaget terms the 'pre-operational' stage. In the case of Bruner, movement is central to the 'enactive' level of knowing, from which the child eventually develops increasingly abstract ways of thinking through the 'iconic' and 'symbolic' levels of knowing (Lawton 1973). The importance of movement-related forms of knowledge is also reflected in Bloom's *Taxonomy of Educational Objectives* (1956, 1964) where, amongst his three 'domains' of development, he includes the 'psychomotor', which has to do with manipulative, motor skills.

EMPHASIS ON MUSIC AND MOVEMENT IN THE WRITINGS OF VARIOUS EDUCATIONALISTS

Music educators have placed varying emphasis on movement in their teaching. For most, its principle role has been to cultivate a sensitive response to music and a feeling for its rhythm and expressive character (Shiobara 1994). Kodály uses movements, in the form of hand signs, to provide a visual representation of pitch (Choksy 1974). Orff sees movement, together with dance and speech, as being very closely related to music (Keetman 1974). Suzuki uses movement to reduce tension. Carabo-Cone uses it to make the process of learning notation more attractive to children. Ward uses movements to cultivate a feeling for musical rhythm and expressive gesture to fix correct pitch in singing (Berry 1976). Willems (Chapius undated) uses physical gesture to articulate a feeling for music and its rhythm, while Jacques-Dalcroze uses it to develop greater self-expression (Dobbs in Simpson 1976).

Such ideas and approaches have been further developed in recent years by Odam, Kemp, Taylor and Shiobara. In the second chapter of *The Sounding Symbol* (1995), George Odam presents a very useful overview of recent research into brain function and what this reveals about the relevance of movement to learning. In this he refers to the fact that the brain is divided in two hemispheres, interconnected through a wide band of nerve cells, the 'corpus callosum'. One side of the brain operates the opposite side of the body so that, for example, the right arm or ear are governed by the left side of the brain. In most people the left brain hemisphere is associated with analytical thought while the right is associated more with feelings and emotions, the affective aspects of our make-up. Movement, on the other hand, is too important for our survival to be confined to one area of the cortex. Instead, it is associated with the base of the cerebellum, the first part of the brain to develop, and it connects to both hemispheres. As a result of this, movement plays a fundamental role and there is evidence that humans develop sophisticated thought processes in both the left and right brain only through movement. Music education is particularly useful in enhancing cross-lateral thinking (more so than science, for example).

The relationship between movement and right brain functions are particularly important. Odam illustrates this with reference to performers. The best performers do not learn to play pieces through a process of logical analysis but through a combination of repetitive movements and an emphasis on contour and aural perception, properties most closely associated with the right side of the brain. This helps stimulate the long term memory from where 'information can be retrieved and examined, deconstructed and analysed at will' (Odam, op. cit., p.14).

This supports the view of Kemp (1990). Drawing on a wide range of research findings, Kemp argues that musical 'knowing' is based on a whole body experience, involving the interrelationship between muscular, perceptual and cognitive behaviour. The memory traces we build of music are not confined to the sound. They also include memory of the neuromuscular sensation of producing the sound. Thus the feeling of the physical gesture of producing a sound is an integral part of the memory of that sound. This is important when it comes to performance. Kemp illustrates this with reference to a child with a beater in the right who is about to produce a sound on a suspended cymbal in the left hand. The child makes a wide circular sweep with the right hand. The kinaesthetic sensation of doing so evokes images of the sound from similar experiences in the past and the qualities of the sound are 'anticipated (imaged) as a direct response to the gesture itself. Furthermore, the quality of the sound is directly determined by a complex interaction between the size of the arc and the velocity of the movement.' In this whole process, highly complex decision-making is taking place which Kemp terms 'body-thinking'. This body-based decision-making is central to performance and, if it is neglected or underdeveloped, performances become unmusical. If children are to develop musicianship and imaginative performance, it is essential to encourage them to imagine in advance of producing the sound.

This has important implications for early years teaching in music. The internalised vision of a piece that a child has will have its foundation in that child's earliest experiences of gestural/musical activities. Kemp illustrates this being put into action in instrumental and vocal activities as well as through involvement in music technology.

It is not only in the early years that movement is relevant to the development of musical memory, as Taylor (1989) has demonstrated in an experiment involving 11–12 year olds. Seventy-two boys and girls were selected at random from a Year 7 group and divided into a control and experimental group. Both groups were given the same amount of exposure to the same set of music items, the same environmental conditions and the same ordering of items. Both groups were asked to listen to a selection of pieces, ranging from jazz through Western classical music to the Indian tradition, with a view to conveying the import of the music to a deaf child. The control group jotted down words to help them remember the music, while the experimental group used movements. When the children were given a subsequent recognition test, it was found that those who had used physical movement and gesture (kinaesthetic strategy) were significantly better at recognising and retaining musical information.

Similar results were found by Shiobara (1994) in her work with 7–8 year olds in the UK and Japan. As part of this research, several pairs of different but similar passages of music were played to the children. They were asked to interpret one extract in a pair through drawing and the other through movement. In individual structured interviews, the extracts were played again and the children were asked to 'describe' what they heard, using a series of cards to 'tell the story of the music'. It was found that there was more detail in the children's descriptions of the music to which they had moved than in the descriptions of the pieces to which they had responded through drawing. One possible reason for this is that movement is more like music than drawing. Movement, like music makes use of time, weight, pace and forward flow and therefore helped the children to focus on the same properties in the pieces which they heard.

IMPLICATIONS FOR MUSIC TEACHING

As we have already indicated, infant teachers have traditionally made considerable use of movement, particularly to help develop concepts of duration. Its relevance to the development of other musical concepts, however, has not been so generally recognised. The rest of this chapter will therefore focus on examples of classroom activity in which movement is used to help develop children's command of a range of musical concepts.

Example 1: beat and dynamics

Children in a nursery class are singing a lullaby. As they do so, some sway their whole bodies to the music; others rock backwards and forwards in a sitting position. One or two are pretending to be rocking a baby brother or sister to sleep. Another is rocking a doll from the home corner. The degree to which their movements match the actual beat of the music varies in 'accuracy' but the fact that they are moving in this way and are pretending to be getting someone to sleep results in their singing more softly than they did in the previous song which was about animals and the sounds that they make. Therefore, the movement seems to have some relationship to dynamics as well as to beat.

Example 2: beat and pitch

In a reception class, children are singing a song about a cobbler mending shoes:

> Cobbler, cobbler mend my shoe.
> Get it done by half past two.
> Stitch it up and stitch it down
> And I'll give you half a crown.

As they sing the first two lines, they pretend to hammer nails in time to the beat of the music. It is interesting to see that some children's movements are twice as fast as those of their class mates. One child does not always keep a steady beat. At times his movements correspond more closely to the rhythm of the words, so that some movements are steady and others are faster or slower. There is a range of abilities and responses here. On the third line, the children pretend to be stitching the leather. On the words 'stitch it up', the melody rises and the children make upward movements. On the words 'stitch it down, the melody falls and the children's movements also go down. In this lesson, therefore, movements are being used to reinforce melody as well as beat.

Example 3: differentiated activities to support the development of beat

The teacher of a mixed Y1/Y2 class has discovered, through observation, that there is a range of responses within her class when children try to make movements to the underlying beat of the music. Some can maintain the beat while beating the time on their laps but have difficulty in marching in time to a beat. Others find it easier to move their whole bodies or their arms in time to the beat. She has therefore planned a lesson which caters for these different levels of ability. The class is singing 'Hickory Dickory Dock' and adding movements to it. Some are sitting on the floor and tapping the beat out on their laps. Others are pretending to be the pendulum of the clock. A third group are pretending to be mice, moving furtively in time around the clock.

Next time she performs the song, the teacher asks some children to produce more complex actions than they did before and two or three of those who can maintain the beat accurately are given unpitched percussion instruments and to transfer their movements onto these. Thus, a child who has been maintaining the beat by tapping his lap is now given a tambour to tap. Another who is pretending to be a pendulum is given a pair of maracas which he holds loosely in his hands. As he sways, they sound in time to the music. Finally, two children who can move very effectively in a variety of ways are asked to play instruments in a more conventional way, without recourse to large body movement. One plays a triangle sound on each beat while the other plays alternating low and high pitched sounds on a wooden agogo.

The use which the teacher makes of movement in these activities shows a clear concern for progression and differentiation.

Example 4: tempo

A class of Y1 children are singing a song about a train which goes up a hill and then down again. As they sing, they pretend to be the train and change the speed of their movements accordingly.

Example 5: tempo

The teacher of a Y2 class marks out the beat of a song. The class copy this and then sing the song while also marking the beat. The song is sung again. This time, the teacher draws attention to the fact that the beat is quicker than last time. The children copy the tempo of the new beat and the children repeat the song and feel the impact of a change in speed on it.

Example 6: accent

In a Y1 class, the children are kneeling in a circle on the floor, facing towards the centre of the circle. They start to sing a two beat African song: 'We We o We Igoniama'. As they do so, they beat the time on their laps. Later, they perform different actions to the song by leaning forward and slapping the floor on the first beat and tapping their laps on the second.

On a later occasion, the children sing another simple two beat song. This time, they mark the beats with alternating movements: clap, tap, clap, tap, and so on. From there, they progress to singing a song in which they pretend to push a friend on a swing. To give the impression that they are pushing the swing into the air, they lean forward on the first beat of each bar. In so doing they are feeling the difference between accented and unaccented notes.

The same approach is applied to a performance of 'Row, Row, Row Your Boat'. As they sing, the children pretend to pull heavily back on their oars on the first beat each time and then move forward more gently on the second beat. The teacher adds further emphasis to the first beat by beating a drum each time it occurs. Later, the children take turns in playing the drum.

Towards the end of Key Stage 1, these children will progress to accenting beats in metres of three and four. When singing a three-beat metre for example, they might produce the following movements using their knees and hands:

Slap–Clap–Clap
or
Slap–Clap–Snap

In each case, the children are developing their understanding of accent through movement. This will help them at a later point if they ever come to examine the theory of music. They will know that the first beat in a bar is accented and that the last beat in a metre of three is the weakest, not because they have been told this in a book but because they will have actually felt the difference.

Example 7: pitch

A class of Reception children is singing a song about a teddy bear who is reaching up high and bending down low. They accompany their movements with appropriate movements: high stretches or patting of the floor.

In a Y1 class, pupils are singing a more complicated song about reaching high, going down low and staying in the middle. Again they accompany their singing with appropriate movements to match the levels referred to in the song. Later, they play a game. The teacher has two chimebars – the highest and lowest in the set. She puts the highest on a table top and the lowest on the floor. The children face the teacher. As she plays the high bar, the children make a stretching movement. When the low bar is played, they bend down to the floor. If a sound is repeated, they keep the physical level but change the nature of the movement. The first time the note is sounded a child might reach up with one hand. When the note is repeated, that child might reach into the air with both hands.

Later, the same game is played but, this time, the children have their backs to the chimebars and have to use their ears to decide how to react. Later still, the same activities are performed with a third chimebar being placed at a middle level, between the high and low notes. A further development involves asking three children to stand in line. Each one makes a particular shape: high, low or middle. Another child then has to decide what order to play the pitches of the notes.

In another school, a mixed age class of infant children is singing a song. As they do so, they trace the contour of the melody with their hands, to show how the musical pitches rise and fall.

In each case, the shape of melodies and differences in pitch are being felt as well as being thought of by the children.

Example 8: phrasing

A class of 6-year olds is being taught a song. The children are standing, with their hands held out in front of them. As they sing a phrase of music, they raise and lower their hands. Some also map out the rise and fall of the melody as they do so. They are learning to feel the shape of the music and to control their breathing to give added emphasis to that shape.

Example 9: volume

A class of Reception children sings a song which has contrasting loud and soft sections. They move to the beat of the music. In the loud sections they make large gestures while, in the soft sections, their movements are less exaggerated.

Later, the children sit in a circle with an instrument each. At a signal from the teacher, they begin to play softly on their instruments. Then, when the teacher makes exaggerated movements, the children make loud sound and, when they see more restrained movements, they play softly again.

Example 10: form

A class of Y2 children listen to a recording of music which has three sections, the first and last of which are the same. When they hear the same music, they must make the same movements. When the contrasting section is played, the movements must be adapted accordingly.

At a later point, the children sit in a circle. Each child has an instrument. Two children stay out of the circle. One has been asked to produce quick, jerky movements; the other to produce slow smooth movements. Each child takes a turn in producing the movements. The rest of the class then play their instruments in a way which matches the movements. The two children then take turns in performing. The pattern of these turns is varied. Sometimes the overall shape is:

Child 1–Child 2–Child 1
At other times it might be

Child 1–Child 2
or
Child 2–Child 1
or
Child 1–Child 1 and 2 together–Child 2–Child 1

In each case, the children are involved in exploring musical forms through movement.

The last example also gives the children a preliminary experience of exploring texture through movement, since more than one idea is being explored at the same time. Movement can also be used to develop notation skills, as will be seen in Chapter 9. The above examples, it is hoped, will give some indication of how movement can be applied to the development of musical concepts and will serve to emphasise that movement is an essential and central element in teaching music in the early years and is not simply an optional extra or addendum to it.

Music literacy and the infant child

THE NEGLECT OF MUSIC LITERACY

For the last thirty years, the development of musical literacy has tended to be neglected in primary schools. Both the Plowden Report (1967) and the Reading University/Schools Council Project (1971), reported in Bentley (1975), indicated that it was given low priority by primary school teachers. This finding was supported by Pugh (1980) who suggested that it was partly the result of a lack of notational expertise amongst primary class teachers. Terry (1994), on the other hand, pointed to time constraints as a reason for notation not being introduced at this level. This is very different from the situation in the late nineteenth century. Soon after the passing of the 1870 Education Act, singing became virtually a compulsory subject in all Board schools, while the Code of 1882 introduced a scheme of 'payment by results' where schools received six pence per pupil for the rote learning of a defined number of songs and a shilling per head if pupils could sing at sight. However, such a situation was short-lived and by 1900, sight-singing had begun to decline as the curriculum widened in scope (Taylor 1979).

Several questions need to be asked. Should music literacy be taught? If so, to whom, at what stage and how? In dealing with early years children, we have to consider very carefully what potential avenues we are opening up through simple, and often apparently rather trite, activities. We help very young children to experiment with objects which float and sink, recognising that, while many will make little progress in science, others might be starting on a pathway that could lead to their inventing a revolutionary type of ocean-going liner. We do not neglect or dismiss these opportunities because they seem too far away from the ultimate goal or because they can only be achieved by some pupils. Thus, the rationale for the inclusion or exclusion of any aspect of the early years curriculum must be viewed against the background of the opportunities made available or denied to the children concerned.

WHY SHOULD WE TEACH MUSIC LITERACY?

We would argue that music literacy is an important element to include in the curriculum since it:

- provides individuals with the means of exploring music independently;
- enables them to formulate their own musical tastes;
- enables them to compose and perform a wide range of complex music.

Musical illiteracy prevents individuals from exploring music for themselves (Pugh 1980). Pointon (1980) disagrees, arguing that we are not denied access to music simply because we cannot read it, since we are bombarded by it all the time. Furthermore, literacy will only give us access to a small part of the world's music since most of it is not written down. Terry (1994) adopts a similar stance, and goes on to claim that, since the greater part of the world's music is not notated, any limitations which illiteracy places on us apply only to printed or manuscript copies of music in the Western European tradition. He recognises that, for a variety of reasons, many important works could be neglected in this way, but feels that works which are not performed or recorded will not be published either. To obtain access to them would involve a search through early editions or manuscripts. This, he argues, takes us 'outside music education to the realms of musicology'.

These commentators are, of course, right when they draw attention to the fact that musical life is not dependent on music notation and there are undoubtedly many advantages to the oral/aural tradition. However the case is sometimes overstated. Terry argues that one of its strengths is that it enables students 'to pursue their interest in composition in *an atmosphere of creative freedom*', a viewpoint which is not shared by all commentators in this field. Fletcher (1987), for example, emphasises how Balinese and Indian music – often regarded as allowing greater freedom for the performer than Western music – is in fact regulated by strict laws and the requirement for great technical precision. The whole business of transmitting music from one performer to another via the oral approach can also be a cumbersome and time-consuming process which places limits on what can be learnt and results in far less music being explored than is possible if one sight-reads a whole series of new pieces. Another point often forgotten by proponents of the oral versus the notated tradition is that the former might well have led to the loss of some very fine music. If the Ancient Greeks, Egyptians and the Mayas could produce wonderful poetry, architecture, pottery and paintings, it is likely that they also produced great music. We shall never know because we no longer have the means of gaining access to it. In view of this, Terry's claim that it is only to the Western European musical tradition that we are denied access through illiteracy does not appear well founded.

In Pugh's article the emphasis is on independent exploration of music. There is no doubt that an individual bombarded by sound from the radio and television can indeed explore a vast amount of music. But ultimately the range of what he or she can explore will be determined by others, be they record producers, concert organisers or programme managers. The individual who is musically literate, on the other hand, can explore music which receives no recognition from such quarters. This does not have to be music which was never printed. It could be works by Ivor Novello or Louis Spohr, which were highly acclaimed in their time but have fallen foul of fashion. If various individuals had not been able to explore music other than what was conventionally available, the music of Bach might have been lost to us in the last century and that of Monteverdi or Hildegard von Bingen would not have been re-discovered in the twentieth century. These examples involve independent exploration. (They also involved musicology in a way that is relevant to music education.) By exploring music independently, the musically literate can make up their own minds and therefore exercise a greater degree of independence in developing their personal musical taste – an essential condition for enabling individuals to develop autonomy of thought and action.

One of the great benefits of the invention of musical notation is that it made it possible for composers to create complex musical textures (James 1993; Odam 1995). That is not to say that notational systems themselves do not have their built-in limitations, as several writers have pointed out (for example, Busoni 1911; Cole 1974; Wishart 1977; Vulliamy and Shepherd 1984). However, the extent to which composers can extend and develop their work is likely to be more restricted if they are musically illiterate.

Cole (1974) and Pointon (1980) see notation primarily as an aid to the reproduction rather than the creation of music. This may be so. However, since performance is an important element in music education, the means of deciphering notation must be given due emphasis. It is one of the ways of 'mastering the environment' (Swanwick 1988). If pupils are being educated for a society in which a large proportion of music is notated, then music literacy is a necessary skill (Plummeridge 1991). Such literacy need not be confined to conventional staff notation. However, if this is the system that gives access to the greatest range of available music, then it has a legitimate claim to being at the forefront of the system taught, just as the 'lingua franca' in a multilingual country has primary emphasis.

WHO SHOULD BE TAUGHT TO BE MUSICALLY LITERATE?

If teaching musical literacy is valuable, it should be offered to all children, but not all commentators support this view. Terry (1994) questions the appropriateness of teaching notation to children who come from a family background in which English is not the first language, since this will place undue pressure on them, particularly if they have learning difficulties. He also argues that the idea of notating music might be alien to children from a family background where music is part of an oral tradition such as folk, jazz, bhangra or reggae.

However, this argument can be challenged in several ways. First, access to more than one language often produces a greater flexibility of approach to learning than a monoglot experience. Therefore, the problems of acquiring 'fluency in staff notation in addition to a second alphabetic language' are probably not nearly as great as Terry suggests. Second, even if one approach to music is more in line with a particular set of cultural traditions, this is no reason for focusing on that approach only. We do not have the right to decide that one approach is relevant to some children and to deny them access to another. We should aim to create a balance by equipping children to function musically in a variety of ways. Thus, the child from a family where music is part of an oral tradition can be taught to become literate while another from a tradition based on notation can be taught to improvise. It is not literacy *per se* that limits individuals' abilities to improvise or perform orally transmitted music, but lack of experience in the latter. It could be argued that, for the vast majority of families in this country, the experience of language prior to the 1870 Education Act was primarily an oral one. Would that have been sufficient reason for not teaching more recent generations to read and write? A person belonging to the third generation of literate people within a family can still appreciate and continue to transmit the stories, poems and family or cultural traditions transmitted orally through the generations.

Terry's claim that those with learning difficulties find it almost impossible to learn staff notation if they already have difficulty with the English alphabet is not borne out in our experiences. We have known Chinese children with not a word of English make good progress and relate well to their teachers and other pupils through the Kodály method when communication and progress were virtually at a standstill elsewhere in the curriculum. Children who have great difficulties in reading and writing can be taught to read and write music using the Kodály method, as we have found on more than one occasion. Often the difficulty with less able children is that they feel cheated by being palmed-off with something other than what they see as being a characteristic musical activity. Being helped to understand notation and to apply it practically can be a tremendous incentive to such children. In one school, virtually every member of the school band was in the special educational needs (SEN) unit. These pupils were very adept readers of music and, outside school, were members of an award-winning band. One of the leading instrumentalists in one of the country's leading orchestras spent a considerable part of his school life in a remedial department. Therefore, it would be unwise to limit access to music literacy on the basis of ability or cultural background.

Terry's article also seems to imply that music literacy is only relevant for the specialist. His article is primarily concerned with secondary education, and it is not clear whether he would regard this as relevant to earlier stages. However, at any stage there is a danger of making assumptions about what is relevant or what is likely to be needed by an individual. We do not have enough data on the effects of differential rates of progress, background, or likely patterns in development of interest, to be able to risk closing down options. This is even more of an issue where early years education is concerned. If we do not give children opportunities at that stage, they will never be in a position of exercising a *real* choice, as opposed to an apparent choice made within the confines imposed by a particular set of circumstances.

Our answer, therefore, to the question 'who should be taught music literacy?' is 'everybody'.

WHEN SHOULD MUSIC LITERACY BE INTRODUCED

If we accept that music literacy should be taught to everybody, then we must decide at what stage this should happen. Again, there are varying views on this. Odam (1995) sees 11 years' old as 'a useful watershed for notation teaching' and argues that at earlier stages it is completely unnecessary, and probably harmful, to encourage them to write anything down using formal systems. On the other hand, Terry (1994) seems to argue that it is because it has been neglected at primary level that the task of presenting it at KS3 is well-nigh impossible.

Literacy of any type takes time to acquire and involves repeated practice. Therefore, the earlier it is started the better. It is clear from the number of children who can read music long before the age of 11, that it is perfectly possible to learn it from an early age. We would not expect much progress in general literacy if we delayed it until 11. Therefore, why should we expect it to be appropriate to music literacy? It could be argued that the curriculum is too full to give attention to literacy and that we may need to slim it down. However, it does not follow that literacy should necessarily be the first element to be jettisoned. The other alternative is to spread the process over a longer period. It is far easier to accommodate literacy if it is introduced earlier. Another crucial factor is the way that music literacy is taught. It can be a central element pursued in an active way and not the theoretical adjunct to which it is too often reduced in schools. Therefore, the next question is to consider how it ought to be taught.

HOW SHOULD MUSIC LITERACY BE TAUGHT?

The problem of how to enable children to read music notation goes back at least as far as the eleventh century when Guido d'Arezzo wrestled with ways of enabling the choristers at the monastery of Pompona, Italy, to read music quickly and easily (Read 1964; Scholes 1972). Guido solved the problem by the use of syllables to represent the sounds of the 'hexachord', or six note scale. By relating each sound to a particular position on the hand, he was able to provide singers with a simple, portable aid to sight singing. His method attracted the attention of Pope John XX, who gave it his support and blessing. Interest in simplifying the learning process through the use of syllables continued even after the five line staff became common. Not all those who tried to deal with the issue were themselves musicians or had primarily musical aims in embarking on the task. Simpson (1976, p.17) suggests that Rousseau's interest in this subject was aroused by his own weakness as a music reader. The method established by Pierre Galin in the late eighteenth century was certainly the result of his inability to master established notation (Simpson, 1976, p.20). John Curwen, a Victorian Congregational Minister, was prompted by the desire to enable his pupils to read music, so that they could improve the standard of singing in church and chapel services. His method of teaching 'Tonic Sol-fa' (Curwen, 1858) was highly influential, particularly in some parts of the country, such as Yorkshire, Lancashire and Wales, and in the 1950s and 1960s there were many older people in these areas with little formal education, who could put trained music graduates to shame when it came to sight reading. Unfortunately, because of its origins in the education of the working classes and because of a misconception that it was intended to be an alternative to staff notation, rather than an introduction to it, Curwen's method was too readily dismissed by many leading musicians and music educators.

It was only when the Hungarian composer Zoltán Kodály (1882–1967) resurrected and adapted Curwen's approaches and clarified the relationship between it and staff notation that some musicians were prepared to see the value of such approaches. In his own country, Kodály's influence became particularly noticeable after the end of the Second World War, with the establishment of Music Primary Schools. The development of Kodály's approach was allied to his concern to revive the folk music culture of his homeland, a concern which he shared with his compatriot Bartók. Therefore, much of his published method takes Hungarian folk song as its starting point. There is often a tendency for such songs to start with a strong first beat as opposed to the up-beat start which is more common in Western European songs. This is one of the reasons that many British and American educators have tended to adapt the Kodály method rather than implement it in its original form. The process of adaptation has also involved combining Kodály's principles with those of the German composer and teacher Carl Orff, whose work with voices and pitched percussion instruments (described in Keetman 1970) was also very influential, particularly in the 1950s and 1960s. Several British publications for infant schools have been based on Kodály's principles or on a combination of the Kodály–Orff approach, including Russell-Smith (1977a, 1977b), Gamper (1986) and Pugh (1994). Further reference will be made to these materials later.

THE CARABO-CONE APPROACH

To be successful, any system of teaching music literacy should reflect what we know about the way that children learn. The work of Piaget and others suggests that children are helped to develop abstract concepts when they are given opportunities to work with concrete representations of those concepts, with which they can interact through seeing, feeling, listening and moving.

Madeleine Carabo-Cone has applied these principles to the teaching of music literacy, through a sensory-motor approach. It is difficult to do justice to this system in this short description and the reader is urged to refer to the more detailed account provided by Mark (1978, p.128–135). In the Carabo-Cone approach, the classroom is organised so that children are surrounded by the image of the grand staff (or stave): on the wall, on the floor, on the piano, on the teacher's clothes, on the table and so on. The children learn the concepts of 'above', 'below', 'in', 'on', 'in between', 'higher', 'lower', and so on, by stepping or lying on the staff or by placing concrete objects at appropriate points on it. To extend their understanding and help them distinguish between symbols, children are helped to identify the focal points of the grand staff – the top and bottom line of each staff, the 'G' line which runs through the middle of the treble clef sign, the 'F' line which runs between the two dots after the bass clef sign, and the 'middle C' line which is invisible when not in use.

The children are helped to identify the focal points by standing on them or by dropping objects such as bean bags onto them. A child identifying the treble G line might first trace round the clef sign with his or her foot before walking along it. In the case of the bass F line, the child might hop on the two dots above and below the line before walking along it. The act of walking along the line reinforces the left to right orientation necessary for reading music. In another context, the children arrange themselves at various points on the staff to represent the notes of a tune. They then sing the tune and, when the note represented by a particular child is sung, he or she squats down for the length of the sound for that note. Further rhythmic activities involve the children wearing 'note hats' representing various note lengths. Wearing these, the children move along sheets of brightly coloured paper, each representing one beat. A two beat note moves into a two-roomed 'apartment' formed by joining two sheets of paper together. In this way, they are able to relate duration to movement and time and also to build up a concept of the interrelationship between note values. Further activities involve notating music by putting biscuits at appropriate points on the staff on the table.

From large body movements, the children progress to more refined body movements, for example using the five fingers of one hand to represent the lines and the gaps between them to represent the spaces of the staff. As they sing, they stroke the lines or poke their fingers into the spaces which correspond with the pitch of the notes being performed.

Through such activities, children progress from the concrete to the abstract and gain experience both of reading and writing music. They also learn notation as part of the process of making music and not as an activity separated from it.

THE ADVANTAGES OF SOLMISATION SYLLABLES AND THE 'MOVEABLE DOH'

The same is true of the Kodály approach. A further advantage of this approach is the use it makes of 'solmisation syllables'. As has already been seen, one of the arguments against teaching notation is the time which it takes. The more that children can transfer the skills which they acquire to new contexts, the quicker the learning process will be.

To illustrate this, consider the scale of C major. This consists of eight notes: C D E F G A B C'. Anyone wanting to read and sing all the intervals in this scale will need to master a number of permutations. For example, from C it is possible to progress to D, E, F, G, A, B, C'. It is also possible to reverse each of these intervals and sing downwards progressions C'–C; B–C, A–C etc. The full range of possibilities within one octave of C major is shown in the following diagram:

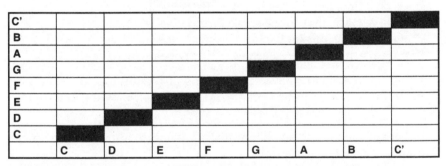

Figure 9.1 The full range of possible intervals in one octave of the C major scale

In all, there are 56 possible intervallic combinations within an octave of a major scale. In addition to C major, there are 14 further major scales:

G major   D major   A major   E major   B major   F# major
C# major   F major   B♭ major   E♭ major   A♭ major   D♭ major
G♭ major   and C♭ major

Therefore, anyone wanting to be able to sing all the intervals up and down within the octave of all the major scales will need to learn 15 × 56 = 840 permutations. Minor scales and singing between octaves would, of course, increase the numbers of permutations even further. A person with perfect pitch would not experience difficulties; but our main concern is with the majority who do not enjoy that advantage.

To rationalise the learning process, therefore, there is a need to identify the similarities between intervals. The relative distance between F# and A# is essentially the same as that between E♭ and G. However, a child would not be able to guess this when the pairs of notes differ entirely from each other, both in their letter names and the symbols (# and ♭) attached to them.

To overcome this problem, the Kodály system uses one set of syllables for the notes of the scale. Thus the ascending notes of all major scales, regardless of which pitch on the piano they start from, will be called:

doh	ray	mi	fa	so	la	ti	doh'
d	**r**	**m**	**f**	**s**	**l**	**t**	**d'**

Once children can sing the relative distance from **s** to **m**, for example, they can sing it in any key and can therefore sing the following:

G–E; C#–A#; A–F#; B♭–G and many more.

Once children know that the first note is **s**, it is easy for them to identify **m** using the following 4 simple rules:

If **s** is on a line, **m** is on the line directly below it;
If **s** is in a space, **m** is in the space directly below it;
If **m** is on a line, **d** is on the line directly below it;
If **m** is in a space, **d** is in the space directly below it.

All that remains is to have some means of identifying the 'doh' in a piece of music. This can be done by applying the following rules when examining the key signature:

If the last sharp of the key signature is on a line, **d'** is in the space immediately above it (see example 1).

Example 1

If the last sharp of the key signature is in a space, **d'** is on the line immediately above it (see example 2).

Example 2

d'   d'   d'   d'

If the last flat of the key signature is on a line, **m** is in the space directly below it (see example 3).

Example 3

m   m   m   m

If the last flat of the key signature is in a space, **m** is on the line directly below it (see example 4).

Example 4

m   m   m   m

As can be seen, this approach enables an individual to sight read music in any of the clefs in common usage in Western music. To learn to sight read all the intervals in the major scales in each clef separately would require the learning of $840 \times 4 = 3{,}360$.

SEQUENCING THE TEACHING OF NOTATION

Approaching music reading through the use of solmisation syllables, as the Kodály method does, is therefore ultimately a very efficient way of learning to sight read, and in the early years provides a firm foundation for future development. Let us now examine a sequence of activities, based on a combination of the Kodály and Orff, which we have used to approach music reading in the infant years. This approach also relies heavily on the work of Choksy (1974), Russell-Smith (1977a, 1977b) and Gamper (1986) particularly.

Like the Carabo-Cone approach, the emphasis is on progression from the concrete to the abstract and from the known to the unknown, with the process of reading and writing being applied meaningfully to practical music-making situations. The emphasis is on letting the experience of sound precede the use of signs and the sequence of activities reflects those involved in the teaching of reading and writing. For reasons explored in Chapter 8, it also makes use of movement.

NOTATION OF PITCH AND RHYTHM

Building a repertoire of songs

Before embarking on the learning of notation, children must first have considerable experience of singing a wide range of rhymes and songs, and of listening and making up their own music. This is the equivalent of giving children wide experience of language through talking; reading stories to them; making up stories for them; letting them make up their own stories; and initiating discussion with adults or each other. Thus the starting point is one of oral/aural experience.

Among the songs taught to them by rote will be simple songs which have been included because later they will be used as particular foci for the development of music literacy. These will tend to be short songs based on two or three pitches (la, so, mi) and very simple rhythms which use one beat and half beat notes. Examples might include the traditional American children's song 'Rain, Rain, Go Away' (s–m) or the English nursery rhyme 'Bye Baby Bunting', or two or three note settings of a well-known nursery rhyme made up by the teacher. As they sing the songs, the children sway, tap or step to the beat of the songs. They perform them loudly or softly, sometimes slowly and at other times more quickly, so that they get used to them and also in order to begin to develop some expression in their singing.

Echo-clapping activities

As part of the preliminary activities, the children will also play simple echo clapping games. For example, with the children sitting in a circle, the teacher might set a metronome ticking and ask the children to tap gently in time to it. The teacher claps out a very simple pattern twice and asks individual children to clap it back to him. This is done in time to the metronome beat. As soon as the individual child has clapped the rhythm, the whole class then claps it. This approach ensures that everyone is involved. At the same time, the complexity of the pattern can be matched to the abilities of individual children, so that the work is appropriately differentiated.

Another version of the rhythmic echoing game involves asking the children to tap in time to a metronome beat as before. This time, the teacher chants out a sentence such as this ' For my breakfast I had toast'. The class repeat the words and the rhythm. Then the process is repeated, this time with the children clapping the rhythm of 'toast'. The sentence is repeated but this time, instead of 'toast', the children have to repeat and copy the rhythm of 'cornflakes' or 'orange juice' and so on. From here the children progress to making up their own breakfast menus or to chanting what they had for tea, what they had for Christmas and so on, so that they are given regular but varied practice at the activity.

Introducing pictures of varying sizes to represent varying note-lengths

At a later stage, the teacher assumes the lead again, telling the children what he had for breakfast. However, this time, he introduces pictures of the objects concerned. For 'toast', he will show a card with one large picture of a single piece of toast. For 'coffee' he will show two pictures to correspond to the two syllables of the word. For 'orange juice', however, he will introduce three pictures of orange juice glasses. The first two will be small and the third will be tall, to correspond with the length of the syllables.

Using pictures to convert signs into sounds and sounds into signs

Later the teacher mounts several of the pictures on separate cards and the children arrange them and clap the words. Then they take turns in rearranging them and clapping the new patterns. This represents a pre-reading process where the children are selecting and reading their own simple rhythms. The same materials can also be used to provide pre-writing experiences. Here the teacher claps the rhythm of the word for one of the foods mentioned and the children have to identify which pictures should be used. Later the separate pictures can be used to 'write' new simple rhythmic patterns made up by the teacher or, in some instances, by the pupils themselves.

Indicating melodic contour through hand signs and other movements

From the time the songs are first taught by rote to the children, the teacher indicates the contour of the melody by raising and lowering his hand. From time to time, the children are also encouraged to 'trace' the melody through arm movements in the air. Gradually the teacher draws attention to the fact that the hand signs he is using are actually different in shape as well as being at different heights. The children are now encouraged to use these hand signs themselves when singing the simple two or three note songs.

The next stage involves the children in responding to both pitches and rhythm simultaneously. This is done by taking the large and small pictures as before and putting them at different heights on the display board.

Replacement of words with rhythmic syllables

When they have reached this stage, the teacher begins to replace the words of the song with rhythm sounds. For example, instead of singing 'Rain, rain, go away' they now sing:

da	da	di-di	da
di-di	di-di	di-di	da

As they sing the song to these rhythmic syllables, they march on the spot. When they have learnt to do this accurately, the children's attention is drawn to the fact that when a **da** is sung, there is one sound to one beat of the foot. On the other hand, when they sing **di-di**, there are two sounds to a foot beat. The children can now play games using these symbols.

Combining body shapes with rhythmic syllables

One very popular game, adapted from Geoffrey Russell Smith, is to ask eight children to stand in line, with their feet together, facing the class. Each child in the line, the teacher explains, is a **da**. The teacher then walks in front of the children from left to right at a steady pace, with each footstep being placed just in front of each child. As she does so, the class chant out:

da   da   da   da   da   da   da   da

The children take turns at being notes and eventually at marching in front of the notes. The next stage is for the teacher to ask some children to stand with their feet apart. The activity is repeated as before but this time, when the teacher steps in front of a child with outspread feet, the rest of the class chant out **di-di** because there are two notes to the beat. In Figure 9.2 the children would chant out:

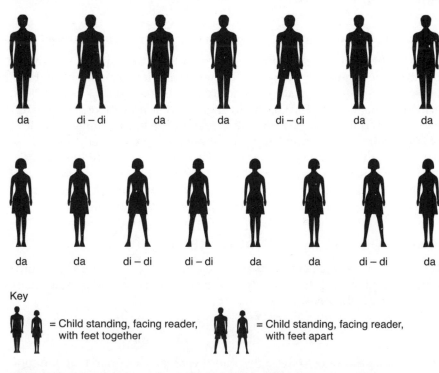

Key

Figure 9.2 Example of combining body shapes with rhythmic syllables

da	di-di	da	da	da	di-di	da	da
and							
da	da	di-di	di-di	da	da	di-di	da

'Reading' and 'writing' music using rhythmic syllables and body shapes

The teacher now rearranges the children or asks them to decide for themselves whether they want to be one beat or half beat notes. The rest of the class then read the new pattern and clap it out, as they chant the syllables. The class can also use their new skills to 'write down' rhythmic patterns. The teacher first claps a simple pattern based on combinations of one beat and half beat notes and asks the children to clap it back. When the pattern is being correctly echoed, the teacher asks one of the pupils to arrange a group of classmates into correct visual equivalents of the pattern. When this has been done, the class once more claps the pattern to check that the written version is correct.

Introducing pitch syllables and using these in 'reading' and 'writing' activities

At about the same time, the children are introduced to the syllables **so** and **mi** and they use these instead of words to sing one of the simple songs in their repertoire. As they do so, they use the two hand signs. The teacher then uses various combinations of the hand signs and asks the children to sing them back to her. It is important that the singing is well phrased and does not simply become a process of 'barking at hand signs'. As with the earlier echo-clapping, the complexity of the activity can be adapted to the varying abilities of the children in the class.

As well as converting signs into sounds, the children can also convert sounds into signs. To do so, the teacher sings a short sequence based on the two notes. The children sing it back and decide on what hand signs should be used. They can then select and arrange a succession of **so** and **mi** cards in an appropriate sequence before singing the phrase again to check on the accuracy of the notation. Other note pitches and note lengths can gradually be added using this approach.

Making the transition to more conventional notation

There comes a point, however, where the children need to be helped to use more conventional notation. In the case of the rhythmic element, this is done by using cards with pictures of children standing in the pose for one or half beat notes and playing the reading and writing games with those before introducing the following symbols:

| = 1 beat = da

⨅ = 2 × half beats = di-di

The children can then repeat the activities and add other note lengths and symbols. Each note length will be introduced in the same sequence:

- learning of song which incorporates the note length;
- focusing on the specific note length;
- playing reading and writing games using body representation of the note length;
- playing the game using picture cards which can be rearranged into a variety of patterns;
- introducing more conventional representations of the note length, again on cards which can be combined in a number of ways for reading and writing purposes.

In the case of pitch, the children will be shown a two-line staff on a felt board. The teacher places a polystyrene note on the upper line. This is **so**. If **so** is on the line, the children are told, **mi** goes on the line immediately below it. It is very easy now to play the game of converting sounds into signs and signs into sounds using the staff and note heads. Later, a third staff line is introduced and the children are given practice in moving the positions and actual pitch of **so** and **mi**, while still maintaining the relative pitch. Through the introduction of a fourth line, they are helped to grasp the notion that if **so** is in a space, **mi** goes in the space below it.

The basis has now been set for them to be able to add more and more notes, to practise using them to read and write, using conventional notation. All that remains is to bring the rhythm and pitch elements together. This can be done by notating the pitches on the staff with the rhythmic notation below them to begin with. Then felt versions of the note stems can be used to determine whether notes are one or half a beat in length and, when two-beat notes are introduced, circles are used to represent the white notes. From here it is an easy step to enabling the children to write notes on the chalk board on laminated charts or on manuscript paper.

The activities described above take place over three years. Although elementary, they provide a basis for further development at Key Stage 2 and beyond, and do not lead the children up the cul-de-sacs of learning which, as Fletcher (1987) has warned, can be a danger with so many 'elementary activities'. It must be emphasised that these are only part of the music programme. While notation work is being pursued, the children also need to have experience of making up their own music, listening to a wider range of music and learning further songs by rote. This is the equivalent of giving children continued experiences of speaking and listening, and extending their oral and aural vocabulary in English, even when their reading and writing skills might be confined to a small number of words.

To ensure that the notation activities are a means to an end and not an end in themselves, they will also need to be integrated into the activities of performing, listening and performing. For example, a child can decipher and play a simple rhythmic ostinato as an accompaniment to a song sung by the whole class. Children who can play the following simple pattern:

could use it to provide an unpitched percussion accompaniment while listening to the second movement of Beethoven's Seventh Symphony. Similarly, children who can sing and recognise the melodic pattern:

m   d   r   m   d   r

can listen for its appearance and reappearance in a performance of 'Carillon' from Bizet's *L'Arlesienne Suite*.

There has been space to give no more than an outline of one possible approach to the teaching of notation to young children. It is an approach that certainly works in helping children to become musically literate, a skill we feel we have no right to deny any child.

GRAPHIC NOTATION

In this chapter, we have deliberately focused on presenting an approach which will eventually enable the child to read and write staff notation. However, as was indicated earlier, this is not the only way to notate music. In the twentieth century particularly, the range of techniques and resources used by composers has extended dramatically, and the sounds produced cannot always be adequately represented in staff notation form. The same holds true for children's compositions, especially where their compositions arise from the exploration of new timbre effects, make use of notes of indeterminate duration or rely on improvisation. Side by side with the activities described above, therefore, it is important to give children frequent opportunities to devise their own notations and produce graphic scores.

As with the teaching of 'conventional' notation, these can be used to enable the children not only to record and reproduce their own compositions but also to enable them to produce scores for others to play. Through listening and discussion, they can then decide how close an interpretation is to the original intention and to reflect on the extent to which their graphic scores have contributed to, or detracted from, this. The graphic scores published in music books and courses for the early years can also be used to enable the children to gain further experience of performance.

We are not advocating the use of solfa and staff notation to the exclusion of all other forms of notation, since the latter are also part of the important process of helping children to become musically literate.

Chapter 10

Music and technology

OVERCOMING BARRIERS TO THE USE OF TECHNOLOGY

Many OFSTED reports have criticised schools for their lack of technology provision in music. This is despite the emphasis which has been placed on it in the National Curriculum.

Hennessy (1995) suggests several possible reasons for this including:

- a lack of staff expertise;
- the high cost of equipment;
- a lack of connection in teachers' minds between computer technology and the creativity, sensitivity and expression expected of music;
- a perception that the individual or small group work associated with computers is ill-suited to a collective activity such as music;
- a tendency to relate computer work to the core subjects rather than the arts areas of the curriculum;
- the limited range of available music software.

She also refers to the evidence of Corber, Hargreaves and Colley (1993 in Hennessey 1995) which suggests that computer technology has a strong masculine image. This might be discouraging to primary teachers who are mainly women and to a subject which, at primary level at least, tends to have a feminine image.

In view of this, it is important to examine the types of technology which are available for music and how these can be used in the infant classroom. The main areas of application involve keyboards, tape recorders, and computers, and in the following paragraphs we will examine aspects of each of these. First, however, it is important to emphasise that technology should be a means to an end and not an end in itself. Too often, schools invest in a particular computer program, for example, and make little attempt to consider how it can be integrated into the overall scheme of work. Instead of being used to develop and enhance children's knowledge, skills or understanding, it becomes an unrelated addendum to activities. For each area of technology, therefore, we will try to highlight its relevance to the central activities of composing, listening and performing and to the body of knowledge and skills which support those activities.

KEYBOARDS

The item of music technology equipment most often found in infant schools is a keyboard. This instrument owes its origin to the search by mid-twentieth century composers for ways of extending the sound palette available to them. As a result of this, it is an ideal medium for helping young children explore the element of **timbre**. In the case of multi-timbral keyboards, it is possible to play several different sounds at once and this enables children not only to explore tone colour but also ways of combining sounds into simple **textures**. Keyboards also help develop concepts of **pitch, tempo dynamics** and **rhythm**. Most have a number of pre-set rhythms, but those which enable children to make up their own rhythms, by using the keyboard like a drum machine, are the most useful in developing relevant skills and understanding.

A simple rhythmic or melodic pattern played by children on the keyboard can make an interesting accompaniment to the **performance** of a song. They can also be taught to reproduce a simple tune, to select a particular timbre and play it against a set rhythm. This will produce a far more exciting effect than the same melody played as a single line on a pitched percussion instrument, for example. The whole process of exploring and talking about the sounds and discussing which ones should be accepted or rejected also involves children in **listening** and **appraising**. But probably the most useful application of the keyboard in the infant classroom is in **composition** activities, as we will try to show in the following example.

A class of 6–7-year-olds is working on a composition about a river. In a previous lesson, they have looked at pictures of various types of rivers: narrow streams, cataracts, wide meandering river valleys, etc. They have also listened to a recording of sections of Smetana's *Vltava*, and the teacher has explained and discussed with them how this represents a river on its journey from its source in the mountains to its arrival in Prague. The children have also painted and collected pictures of various types of rivers. They are now working in groups on producing a musical version of the river picture of their choice. Most are working on pitched and unpitched percussion instruments. Three children are working on the keyboard. Their chosen picture is an aerial photograph of the Thames Valley.

They start by experimenting with some very 'unwatery' sounds. When the teacher challenges them about this, they explain that they have decided that, since their picture is taken from the air, they should include the sound of an aeroplane. They are going to fly down towards the river in this. After further experimenting, they decide on a particular setting and increase the volume to represent the swooping of the plane. Then they switch to the river. After much debate, they find a sound for the water but the next problem is to make the transition from one sound to the other. Eventually they produce a very crude transition which involves simply stopping, resetting and starting again. The teacher asks them to play this to the rest of the class.

Their classmates listen fairly patiently but soon identify the lack of continuity from the aeroplane sound to that of the river. This becomes the focus of discussion led by the teacher. Various children make, and demonstrate, suggestions for improving the composition. These tend to focus on changing the timbre and speeding up the transition from one section to the other but the gap in the composition still remains. Eventually, one child suggests that what they need is two sounds, one to represent the plane and one to represent the river. The performers take this to mean producing two sounds simultaneously on the keyboard. But the child explains that what she means is that they should use the keyboard together with another instrument. The others seize on this with enthusiasm and lots of suggestions are made. Finally, it is decided that the river is to be represented by a slow glissando on the alto glockenspiel against the sound of the plane on the keyboard. The original group then carries on with this idea. Eventually, they produce their final version. By this stage the teacher notices that the original great crescendo on the keyboard has been replaced by a shorter crescendo followed by a diminuendo, giving way to the glissando on the glockenspiel which grows gradually louder and then dies away. The piece ends with a very abrupt stopping of the aeroplane engines.

The final piece was by no means the best produced by this group. However, the interesting point was the way that the children took very naturally to combining electronic and non-electronic media. They also realised that the techniques of exploring, discussing, experimenting, refining and finalising which they applied elsewhere in their composition were equally applicable to the process of composing with electronic media.

In this particular case, the children simply performed the composition live. Other children in the class, who had already used the keyboard for composition, had also recorded their pieces using the built-in recording mechanism and were able to play these back. Not all keyboards have an inbuilt recording device and most of the music (electronic or acoustic) recorded in the infant classroom tends to involve the use of the tape recorder.

TAPE RECORDERS

There are several good reasons for recording children's work:

- it enables them to hear what they have produced and to comment on and appraise their own and others' work;
- it provides a record of composition-work in progress, and helps children recall what they have already produced when they are involved in work which spreads over several sessions;
- it enables a teacher to build up a portfolio of evidence which can be used for assessment purposes. This can reflect the process as well as the products of performance and composition work.

However, there can also be disadvantages in the use of tape recordings:

- performances can often sound far less interesting in recorded form than they do when heard live, particularly if the equipment is mediocre. This can be a disincentive to pupils;
- one of the most important skills for musicians to develop is the ability to listen to the overall effect of a performance as well as to their own part. This skill can only be acquired in a live situation and an over-reliance on tape recorders can detract from its development;
- an over-reliance on tape recording can also restrict the development of children's aural memory. As adults, our minds become increasingly cluttered with the detritus of life – remembering when to make tax returns, pay bills, etc. – and to cope with this we become heavily reliant on external aids. The young child is not burdened with these issues and can often remember far more than adults give them credit for. In one class of 7-year-olds, for example, children were able to recall and reproduce each stage in the development of a composition which had taken them four weeks to produce. They did this without recourse to any written or taped prompts. We must be aware of this and not blunt an important faculty through an over-reliance on electronic gadgetry.

If tape recording is to be used, the children must be helped to use the equipment for themselves. Battery tape recorders are probably the safest, although older children can be taught to work safely with electrical equipment, so long as clear procedures are established, with strict codes of supervision. It is also essential, of course, that all equipment is regularly checked for safety by the school's health and safety officer.

One technique for helping children develop independence in the use of tape recorders, while also ensuring that the process is closely supervised, is to appoint 'classroom sound engineers' who have responsibility for recording the work of their classmates for a particular week. Their skills can build up gradually from simply switching the tape recorder off and on at the right time, to setting up and using the equipment independently.

When all children have reached this stage, they will be able to decide for themselves when to use the tape recorder to record part or whole of a composition. This process of deciding what, why and when to record is in itself an important element in the process of building up skills of decision-making and appraising. It also helps with the process of assessment, since each class or group can be given its own tape, which then builds into a portfolio of work to date. This material can then be made part of a display showing how a composition or performance started and developed, through successive stages, to its final form.

So far, our discussion has focused on the use of the tape recorder as a means of keeping a record of compositions and performances. It can also obviously be used as an important resource for listening. As we have emphasised elsewhere, children need to return to a piece again and again if they are to be become familiar with it. A listening centre, with multiple headphones, positioned in one corner of a classroom, can help both individual and group listening and reinforce work pursued as a whole class. Carefully prepared question sheets can help focus the children's attention on specific aspects of what they hear and help prompt further discussion with the teacher or classroom assistant. Using listening centres in this way can also help in the organisation of a class. While some children are listening to recordings and others are discussing the work they have already done or are drawing a graphic score of their compositions, a third group can be involved in practical work with more direct teacher input.

Another application of tape recorders is as a specific instrument in composing. Sounds recorded from nature or the general environment can be interpolated into compositions involving conventional instruments. Tape recorders with changing speed mechanisms can also be used to help change the quality of a sound by playing them at twice or half the speed of the original recording. This extension to the sound spectrum can be as exciting for young children as for older pupils. Another example of tape recorders being used to extend children's sensitivity to timbre involved a teacher recording the voices of all the pupils in class and later using this to help the children identify whose voice was whose. From here, they progressed to identifying the voices of characters on children's television programmes. By asking the children to describe as well as to identify the voices, the teacher also helped them to develop sensitivity to such elements as pitch and speed, as well as sound colour.

Another way of extending the raw material of sound available to children is to use reverb units. These can be set to reproduce the effects of wide echoing spaces or the very dead acoustics of a constricted space. This is an important resource to help children explore ways of producing various atmospheres, particularly when the effects of echo and other types of distortion are used. Young children react well to this type of activity and it should not be delayed until a later point in the educational process, on the mistaken assumption that some types of musical experience are more appropriate for some ages than for others.

COMPUTERS

Computers are what most people think of first when music technology is mentioned although, as we have seen, this is only one type of resource applicable in the classroom.

If computer software is to be used successfully in the classroom, it is essential that the hardware is suitable. Teachers in one infant school were recently disappointed to find that children could not use a software package which focused on the difference between high and low sounds because the volume was too soft for them to be able to hear the differences in pitch. It is important, therefore, to make sure that the school invests in good-quality headphones, speakers and amplifiers, so that the sound reproduced is of sufficient volume and quality to be of interest and use to the children. Making sure that a computer can be linked to a keyboard through a MIDI system and that it can accommodate CD-ROM is also important if the best use is to be made of hardware. Buying the cheapest hardware or not ensuring that various items of equipment are mutually compatible is a false economy and does not give good value for money.

The range of software for music, especially in the early years, is not particularly extensive, although its quality is gradually improving. Many suppliers now operate a system whereby a school can hire software for a trial period before deciding whether or not to borrow it. If such a trial arrangement is to be effective, it is important to make sure that all staff are helped to see the relevance and application of the software concerned. In the case of a school with limited staff expertise, it might be a good investment to buy in consultancy at this particular point, so that an informed decision can be made on whether the equipment is appropriate or not.

As with all other resources, it is important to identify precisely how various items of software can support the central activities of music and help develop children's grasp of relevant contexts. This needs to be clearly reflected in the planning for the subject. Below are examples of the types of software that can be useful for the activities of composing, listening, performing and development of knowledge about music.

Software to support listening activities

Software for listening ranges from packages that focus on identification of sounds to more sophisticated programs that enable the user to listen and analyse the works of established composers.

An example of a program in the first category is *Tuneland*. This includes more than 40 classic children's songs, puzzles and magic tricks which children can access by clicking onto particular points in a scene. One way of integrating this program into other work in a scheme is to use some of the songs on the software as a basis for live vocal work.

Listen to Music is designed to reinforce music listening skills and includes activities which help children discriminate between high or low notes and long/short, loud/soft sounds, etc. The program also focuses to a certain extent on sound textures.

Musical Instruments, as its name implies, features over 200 instruments from all around the world and enables the child to sample 1,500 sounds from a range of instruments, ensembles and styles. The inclusion of 500 photographs of the instruments is another advantage in helping children extend their skills in identifying timbre.

At the other end of the spectrum is *Peter and the Wolf*. This is an interactive program, specifically designed for 4–8-year-olds, which enables the children to follow a video introduction to the story, to relate instruments to their position in the orchestra and to the characters that they represent in the story. It also enables children to learn about the composer and to play a game based on listening activities.

Software to support composition activities

A useful program which combines listening and composing activities, and which is particularly suitable for young children is *Beetles*. This has a special needs and nursery option. The beetles on the screen are programmed to play a wide variety of instruments and tunes and to play these in various combinations, and as lead or backing parts. They can also play tunes made up by the pupils. Thus, the program is very well suited to help develop pupils' grasp of the concepts of timbre and texture, as well as their skills in composition and listening.

Another useful program for developing composition skills is *Compose World*. Here, pictures or words are used to represent musical phrases. These phrases can be of any length and involve both melody and harmony. Children can experiment with them to build up their own compositions. Additional discs or phrase sets and sound modules, which allow for differentiation and progression, are available.

Varying abilities and ages are also catered for by *Rhythm Maker*. With this, children can create one or more rhythmic patterns that can then be sequenced together to make a track. Independent volume and tempo control allow alterations to be made as the track progresses. A number of 'effects' can also be added to each pattern. As with other programmes, this can also be used to enhance children's grasp of concepts, as well as their compositional skills.

A useful set of programs for children from as young as 3 years of age, is

Peter Beater's Music Games. Here children learn the meaning of 'up', 'down', 'the same', and to discriminate between higher, lower and repeated notes. This is done by moving Peter Beater and other characters. There are also open-ended activities where children can experiment freely with pitch and rhythm, compose their own music and hear it played back.

Music Maker comes in two parts. The first of these, *Musical Minibeasts,* is particularly useful for young children. It focuses on pitch and rhythm with tunes being composed using graphics of minibeasts to represent the notes. These can be entered using the keyboard or concept keyboard.

Software to support performing activities

Several of the programs described above can be used to play back children's performances. Programs are also being developed to help children learn to play instruments. One interesting example is *The Recorder.* This helps children of 6 years and above to practise by providing an animated view of the holes on the instrument being opened and closed for each note of a tune. The pupil chooses the speed but can also move from one note to the next using the space bar. Note-reading is taught interactively and background information on the recorder is also included. Another useful feature of the program is a section on composing.

Two other popular programs are *Note Invaders* and *Notate.* These can be useful with the most able children in Key Stage 1 but are probably more applicable to older age groups.

Software to support INSET activities

All the materials described so far can be incorporated into INSET activities or be used to supplement the ideas on staff development presented in Chapter 16. However, *First Class Music* is a software program which has been designed specifically for use in the in-service training of non-specialists. It provides a huge library of resources, including more than 200 activities and 1,000 musical excerpts and 90 print-out worksheet masters.

Application of word processing skills

It is not only for teaching and learning programs of the type described above that computers can be used in music. Older infants can also be encouraged to use their developing word processing skills in a variety of circumstances, including listing the various sounds that they have produced on particular instruments; listing the pieces that they have heard; describing what they liked about them; or describing how they developed a composition of their own.

This chapter has been no more than a brief outline of the ways that music technology can be used in music. To give more details of hard and software is difficult since it tends to change rather rapidly. Nevertheless, we hope that these ideas will be a spur to further thought and help make the subject a little less daunting than it often seems to early years teachers.

Chapter 11

Staffing issues

WHO SHOULD TEACH MUSIC?

In this section, we will focus on the issues of planning and monitoring the music programme. First, however, there is a need to consider who should teach it. The simple answer to this is the class teacher. The class teacher usually teaches the other subjects and areas of learning in the early years curriculum and is therefore able to make the relevant connections between various aspects of the experience presented to the children. Having one teacher for all subjects is less confusing for young children. Working within one set of clearly established routines helps them to build up confidence and to orientate themselves. It is also administratively more convenient and often more efficient for a school to be organised along these lines. The principle of having one teacher for all subjects, however, can break down where music is concerned.

LACK OF CONFIDENCE IN THE TEACHING OF MUSIC

There is considerable evidence to suggest that many teachers lack confidence in their own abilities to teach music. In a survey of 901 teachers, Wragg, Bennett and Carre (1989) showed that the subjects which these people felt least confident about teaching were music and design technology. This confirmed the findings of Mills (1989), who found that the subject which most worried a group of generalist student teachers was music. In its review of primary inspection findings for 1994/5, OFSTED (1996) reported that 'many teachers lack confidence in their ability to teach music and this affects the frequency with which they teach it in their class'.

POSSIBLE REASONS FOR THIS SITUATION

There are several possible reasons for this situation. Mills (1991) suggests that individuals' lack of musical self esteem is partly a reaction to being criticised or excluded from musical activities at school. Another possible factor (Mills 1991, Allen 1988, Hennessy 1995, Durrant and Welch 1995) is the perception which teachers have of what musical activity and music teaching involve. Many think of music teaching as being restricted to the transmission of performance skills and see their own lack of technical competence as a major stumbling block to pursuing musical activities with children. A third factor is the adequacy of the musical training offered to student teachers.

The UK Council for Music Education and Training – UKCMET – (1983) recommended that all intending primary teachers should have a compulsory music element in their course. Despite this, the 1987 DES survey on initial teacher training found a generally inadequate provision for the expressive arts in both BEd and PGCE courses, and a year later Allen (1988) showed that music remained optional in some teacher training courses. Government intervention in teacher education actually led to the decline of provision in some instances. The national survey of teacher education in the late 1980s focused on the 'degree worthiness' of courses. The Criteria for the Assessment of Teacher Education (CATE criteria), adopted at the time, focused on the need for A level as a qualification for studying particular subjects as part of BEd courses. The result was that some institutions had to narrow their range of music courses and limit the opportunities for students to develop their music knowledge, skills and understanding. Since then, further pressures have eroded these opportunities, not least being the allocation of increasing amounts of time to the core subjects in teacher training courses (a requirement which has been re-emphasised in the Teacher Training Agency's revised requirements for Initial Teacher Training (TTA 1997)). The limitations on DfEE allocations of places for training in music and the pressure to reduce the time spent on gaining qualified teacher status have tended to marginalise music even further. The current thrust on the part of the Teacher Training Agency to involve schools more directly in training through partnerships with higher education institutions or through School-Centred Initial Teacher Training Schemes (SCITT) (TTA 1995) also presents problems. The success of these initiatives depends very much on the quality of what is offered within the schools concerned. If initial teacher training students are working within institutions where there is high quality teaching across the curriculum, then there is no problem. However, the difficulty for many higher education institutions is finding such schools and this has an impact on music as for any other subject.

In March 1997, the Music Education Council published a *Manifesto for the Millennium*, which included amongst its targets the demand for:

- sufficient Initial Training Places and INSET support to provide appropriate subject coordination for each Key Stage 1 and Key Stage 2 institution;

- sufficient time to be provided on Initial Teacher Training courses to develop the necessary skills for general classroom teachers to deliver National Curriculum music;
- improvement in teachers' competence, with 100 per cent having a recognised validation of specialist music education through initial or in-service training.

It will be interesting to see what impact this document will have on the development of legislation and policy, both locally and nationally.

THE EFFECTS OF THE CONTENT AND NATURE OF COURSES

Increasing the provision for music will not, in itself, necessarily improve the situation. It will depend on the content and quality of what is offered. In one Australian study, for example, the value which initial teacher training students placed on music and the enjoyment which they gained from it declined over the period of their training course (Gifford 1993). However, this might have been a result of the nature and content of the specific courses concerned. Barrett (1994) describes an action research study in which compulsory music curriculum units for generalist primary and early childhood teacher education students were re-developed to make compositional experience and open-ended challenges the main focus of activity. Qualitative evaluation suggested that the students concerned not only developed musical skills and knowledge and an understanding of a range of teaching and learning strategies, they also felt more capable and confident as musicians.

One way of compensating for the lack of appropriate initial teacher training is to focus on in-service training in music. However, competing demands for time and resources for training in other areas of the curriculum often limit the focus on music. Even where headteachers are committed to its provision, it is not always easy to enthuse the teachers who are most in need of help. The provision of in-house training has gone some way to tackling this problem. As with initial training, the nature and focus of in-service can also be a crucial factor in determining its effectiveness. This and other issues will be examined further in Chapter 16.

MUSIC SPECIALISTS

Schools have adopted a variety of strategies for dealing with teachers' lack of confidence and expertise. In the past, the position varied considerably across the country or even within one neighbourhood. Many schools paid no more than lip-service to the subject and, in some cases, ignored it entirely. Where the subject was given any emphasis, it was often put into the hands of a 'specialist' who was responsible for teaching the subject to the whole school. This was reflected in a number of surveys and reports (for example, DES 1978, 1982 and 1985, cited in Mills 1991). Many of these specialists taught the subject directly to classes rather than acting as advisers to their colleagues, as those with curriculum leadership responsibility in other subjects might have done. Given that they usually had other responsibilities, it was not always possible for them to ensure that all children received a consistent programme throughout their time in the primary school. The disadvantages in terms of continuity and progression are obvious. Music also tended to be taught in isolation from other subjects, even within schools which were great protagonists of 'topic work' and the 'integrated day'.

MUSIC CONSULTANTS

The 1978 DES survey (Allen 1988) suggested that the most suitable person to match the music curriculum to the needs of pupils was the class teacher. This became a fairly popular view in the 1980s and early 1990s. In part, as Allen demonstrates, it was a response to the effects of educational contraction. Falling roles and cuts in expenditure meant that schools could no longer afford the luxury of the old style music specialist. The practice of the teaching music as an integrated element in the curriculum was felt by many to be consistent with a so-called child-centred approach. The notion of class teachers taking responsibility for their own music teaching under the guidance of a 'music consultant' gained considerable support from several quarters (such as DES 1985; DES 'Better Schools' 1988; and, to a certain extent, the Gulbenkian Report of 1982). Many LEAs also invested a great deal of time, effort and money in running music consultancy training, in conjunction with higher education institutions, notably Reading University's Music Education Department.

Unfortunately there was not always sufficient time or the resources for evaluating the effectiveness of these strategies within schools. Allen (1988) conducted a survey in Nottinghamshire schools to determine whether the claims made for music consultancy were as great in practice as its advocates had claimed. For this, he used two questionnaires and a small number of case studies, and focused on the responses of three groups: consultants, specialists and non-specialists. He came to the conclusion that the work of a consultant influenced the overall content of the music curriculum in a more limited way than that of the specialist music teacher, who achieved a more satisfactory provision in terms of breadth and balance. Where music consultancy was successful in terms of producing a satisfactory education for all children, it tended to be the result of several interrelated factors including:

- class teachers having some degree of personal musical skill and experience;
- headteachers being supportive and making available staff time in which to develop the music curriculum;
- other staff valuing music as part of the curriculum and supporting the notion of music consultancy;
- opportunities for INSET, preferably school-based, of consultant and staff;
- the consultant being knowledgeable in music teaching techniques and skills;
- the consultant fully understanding the consultancy role.

The formal training and musical capability of the post-holder seemed to have little bearing on the ability to function successfully as a consultant.

The period since Allen's study has seen major changes in education, not least being the advent of the National Curriculum, the Local Management of Schools and the OFSTED cycle of inspections. Schools no longer have the option of whether or not to teach music. Many of them have had to face undreamed of financial constraints. Fewer schools than ever can afford the luxury of teachers whose primary concern is music. At the same time, the lack of musical expertise among the staff cannot be used as an excuse for not giving children their legal entitlement. Therefore, the emphasis has to be less on ideology and more on pragmatic strategies for ensuring the most efficient way of planning and delivering the curriculum.

Whatever the situation, there is clearly a need – as with any subject – for someone to coordinate the music curriculum and to take responsibility for delivery, either directly or through the provision of guidance and help through planning. How this might be effected is examined in detail in the next section. There is, however, one disturbing development which needs to be highlighted at this point.

Many schools, faced with the need for a music coordinator, tend to appoint staff straight from higher education to the post, confident that such teachers' music qualifications will, in themselves, help overcome the problem. In practice, many of these newly appointed coordinators are faced with several problems. First, as new entrants, they have to focus on the delivery of the curriculum as a whole and to focus on developing their own generic teaching skills before being able to focus on their specific area of expertise. This inevitably leads to a delay in the return on the school's investment and yet another year group misses out on its full entitlement. Furthermore, the lack of general experience saps the confidence of many such teachers in offering advice to more established teachers. In some cases, this is even exploited by older established colleagues who are determined to avoid teaching an area of which they were afraid.

THE ROLE OF THE MUSIC COORDINATOR

If there is to be a coordinator for music, it is essential that he or she performs the same role as coordinators of other subjects. English coordinators do not teach the subject on behalf of their colleagues. They offer advice, direction and guidance, and perform a management role. As with other subjects, the music coordinator should draft relevant documents, oversee any consultation process, revise documents in the light of discussion and present the final versions for approval by the senior management and the governors of the schools. They should also monitor the implementation of the policies and schemes and oversee assessment, recording and reporting.

Ideally, the coordinator should have some musical training. However, there are many trained musicians who have few skills of management and many non-musicians who, because of their management skills, can help develop their own and others' work in music to the obvious benefit of the children in their care.

Whatever staffing a school has, and whatever strategies it adopts to deploy individuals' expertise, it is essential that a long-term view is taken of the situation. Too often, schools appoint musicians to their staff and rely entirely on them until the day comes when they leave to take up another appointment and the whole music provision is once again put in jeopardy. A carefully devised programme of staff development, designed to disseminate the skills of an expert across the rest of the staff, will alleviate such problems. 'Give a man a fish', says the Chinese proverb, 'and he will eat for a day. Teach him to fish and he will eat for a lifetime.' It is on the teaching, rather than the giving, that headteachers and governors need to concentrate.

Chapter 12

Subject development planning and resourcing

THE IMPORTANCE OF PLANNING

In the last few years, there has been increasing emphasis within schools on the production of development plans and on the provision of guidance for this (DES 1989; DES 1991, OFSTED 1994). The documentation has tended to adopt a whole-school perspective on how to improve standards, quality, efficiency and ethos. However, there is also a place for identifying developmental needs for each subject area and in this chapter we shall examine how this might be done for music within an infant school.

Planning is as essential to music as to any other area of the curriculum. Without clear planning we will not know what we are trying to achieve, how we are going to achieve it, when it is to be achieved or whether it has been achieved. Without clear planning, we will not be able to differentiate between what is intended and unintended; between what is relevant and irrelevant; or to know whether or not we are on course. Most important, we will not know whether we are making good and effective use of that most precious commodity – time.

REVIEW OF THE CURRENT SITUATION

The first priority should be to establish what the current situation is in relation to the subject. Below are some examples of the types of questions that could be asked at this stage.

Standards

- What are the standards achieved by the children in music?
- How do these standards compare with attainment in other areas of the curriculum?
- How well do music standards in this school compare with standards locally and nationally?
- How well do children of different abilities perform in music?

Quality

- How effectively is music taught within the school?
- Are all teachers confident in teaching it?
- Is every child taught music or is this time used to remove some children for extra help in reading or other core subject areas?
- Are the children given sufficiently differentiated work in music or do they have to work in large groups because it is the school's policy to combine classes for music?
- Does the school have a music policy? If so, how up-to-date is it?
- Is there a clear scheme of work for music? If so, how good is it? Does it cover the programmes of study in music? Does it allow for progression? Does it have a clear time-scale for delivery of the subject?
- Is there an assessment policy? If so, how good is it?
- Do all teachers use the schemes and policies consistently?
- Is there a system of evaluating the effectiveness of the implementation of the policies and schemes?

Efficiency

- How much time does each class spend on music within a week?
- Is the use of this time clearly planned?
- What resources are there for music?
- How good are these resources? Are they sufficient? Are they in a good state of repair? Are they used regularly? Are they used effectively?
- How much money has the school spent on music in the last three years?
- Is the existing musical expertise of staff used for the benefit of all staff and pupils?
- How much time and money has been invested in staff development in music?
- Has the investment on resources and INSET had any perceivable impact on the children's attainment in music?

Ethos

- What role does music play in the school? Is it confined to classroom activities or does it also have an impact on other aspects of the school's life?
- How is the subject perceived by governors, staff and parents? Is it seen as an important part of the curriculum, an optional extra, an activity for all or only for a few?
- How do the children react to music? Do they respond enthusiastically to it or are they bored by it or indifferent to it?
- When they perform do they do so with confidence?

- When they listen do they do so with concentration?
- When they compose are they full of ideas and ready to explore all kinds of possibilities?

The best way of gleaning this information will vary from school to school, depending on its size, structure and the nature and patterns of relationships among the staff. It could be done through meetings of the whole staff or of year groups, or by means of questionnaires. Whatever approach is adopted, however, it is essential that it produces an honest picture of the situation in a way that challenges staff, without making them feel unduly exposed, threatened or depressed.

There will be some questions which the staff might not feel confident or competent to answer. For example, they might not feel in a position to be able to compare standards in their school with those in other institutions. Information published by OFSTED in its periodic review of inspection findings could help. In addition, the school could call on the advice of external consultants from the Local Education Authority or other relevant organisations in answering these particular questions. Parents' perceptions of their children's musical experiences could also be a very useful contribution to the review process. This is particularly important in view of the Parents' Charter.

DRAWING UP A PLAN

The danger at this stage of the proceedings is that a school identifies so many things wrong with its music provision that it does not know where to start. Alternatively, it might try to tackle all the issues in one go. Clear and realistic priorities that take account not only of the musical needs of the school but also the other areas for development will therefore need to be established. These will, in turn, need to be viewed in relation to the time and money available to the school.

There will be some aspects that can and will need to be addressed ahead of others. These should be the basis of the short-term plan. Others will be included in the longer-term plan for the subject. In drawing up the subject plan, it is important to ensure that

- the priorities reflect the overall aims or mission statement of the school;
- targets are set;
- targets are achievable;
- there is a clearly-defined time-scale for implementation that is realistic and also flexible;
- there are clear success criteria for each target;
- there is a clear timetable for the regular monitoring of progress towards the targets;

- the resources needed – in terms of time, equipment and personnel – are clearly identified;
- any training needs are identified, prioritised and addressed systematically;
- the costs, both in time and money, are clearly identified;
- staff responsible for implementing and overseeing the plan are identified;
- the plan is clearly presented, can be understood by all concerned and is published to all relevant parties, including the governors;
- the intended impact on the quality of learning and pupil attainment is clearly articulated.

Table 12.1 suggests how a subject development plan might be presented.

Each target can then be further broken down to provide more detail, as in Table 12.2.

It is very important to remember that the plan should be a means to an end and not an end in itself. Therefore, it might well need to be updated and adapted in response to changing circumstances. It is also important that in the process of adaptation, the original reasons for including an idea are reviewed, so that its effectiveness is not lost. The plan will need to be updated annually. At this stage, there will need to be a mechanism to ensure that targets are not 'lost' because, for some reason, they have not been met within a defined timescale. OFSTED (1994) highlights this as a common pitfall.

This plan is simply an outline. The subsections of it will need to be expanded further. In the following chapters, we will focus on more detailed planning in relation to:

- the devising of a school music policy;
- drawing up a scheme of work;
- monitoring procedures;
- resourcing music provision.
- staff development needs.

Before that, however, we need to examine the issue of resources.

RESOURCES FOR MUSIC TEACHING

The first review of OFSTED inspection findings (OFSTED 1995) reported that approximately one-third of primary schools were not properly equipped with a suitable range of good quality instruments for performing and composing. There was a particular lack of tuned and bass instruments. A small number of schools was also found to have spent large sums of money on expensive equipment, such as orchestral instruments, which could only be used by a few pupils, or commercial schemes that could not be implemented for the lack of instrumental resources.

Table 12.1 Example of a subject development plan

Target	Time-scale	Costing	Responsibility	Monitored by	Success criteria
1 To improve the composition work being pursued within the school	1998–2000	• GEST funding: £X • Subject Resource allocation: £X • Directed time for all staff: X hours • Directed time for coordinator: X hours	Coordinator, in consultation with HEI and LEA adviser, working with staff	Headteacher	• Clearer indication in scheme of work of what has to be covered and how it is to be done • Teachers have clearer understanding and greater confidence • Composition work occupies 30% of music curriculum in all classes • Standard of composition work increased
2 To extend the range of instruments in all classes	1998–2000	Following expenditure from departmental allocation: 1998–1999: £X 1999–2000: £X 2000–2001: £X	Coordinator	Headteacher	By 1999, all classes to have access to chromatic soprano and alto percussion instruments on a shared basis By 2000, each class to have its own set of unpitched percussion instruments By 2001 all classes to have access to a bass xylophone
3 To extend the use of IT in music classes	1999–2002	1999–2000: Coordinators to attend course on IT and music and disseminate information to rest of staff 2001–2002: INSET and equipment to be purchased to enable staff to develop understanding in this area 2002–2003: IT to be integrated more systematically into scheme of work	Music coordinator and IT coordinator	Deputy head teacher	By 2004, all classes making confident and regular use of IT in the music programme

Table 12.2 Breakdown of a targeted area

Target 1: to improve the composition work being produced within the school

Focus	Target	Time-scale	Responsibility	Costing	Monitored by	Success criteria
Teaching	To revise the scheme to include greater emphasis on composition	Revised scheme completed by beginning of Autumn Term 1998	Coordinator in consultation with staff and LEA adviser	Time: Directed time from 1265 allocation; for revision of scheme and for discussion with whole staff: X hours for coordinator X hours for rest of staff Cost of production and reproduction of draft and final versions: £ X	Headteacher	Teachers have a clearer understanding of what they are to cover when and this is reflected in their practice
Attainment	Improvement of standard of compositions produced by pupils	By beginning of Winter Term 2000	Class teachers	Average of 30% of music time per week to be allocated to composition activities from beginning of Winter Term 1999	Coordinator	Pupils' compositions show greater use of variety of instrumental colours, rhythmic devices and have a greater sense of shape
INSET	INSET course on composition to be attended by coordinator	Spring Term 1998	To be delivered by local HEI	2 Days to be financed from GEST allocation	HEI	Coordinator has clear strategy to revise scheme to include more composition work
	In-house INSET on composition for rest of staff	Autumn Term 1998	Coordinator to deliver	3 × 2 hour twilight sessions	Coordinator	Class teachers' skills and confidence in planning and delivering composition increased
Resources	3 sets of chimebars and chromatic xylophone to extend range of sound sources available	Instruments in place by end of Autumn Term 1998. In use from beginning of following term	Coordinator to order	£X from resources allocation to the subject	Headteacher and coordinator	Every class displays use of pitched and unpitched percussion in compositions

The picture painted by OFSTED is not at all surprising. Traditionally music has been the Cinderella subject where resources are concerned. It is not uncommon to find schools that have not made a systematic investment in instruments for almost ten years. The arrival of the National Curriculum has gone some way to changing headteachers' views, but it has also been used to the further detriment of music. It has been all too easy for schools to argue that they need to spend money on ensuring that the core subjects are in place, even though these subjects have always traditionally taken the greatest slice of the school budget. Even when schools do come to spend money on music, the amount made available is often far too little and does not take account of the accumulated deficit over several years. One reason for this is that headteachers do not always have a realistic notion of precisely how expensive musical resources can be. They are also unaware, in some cases, of the full impact of the changes which have occurred in music education in recent years. Unplanned investment by staff on previous occasions has led, in some instances, to inappropriate resources being bought. The resultant under-use has dissuaded heads from 'throwing good money after bad', especially when their budgets are getting increasingly tighter in many instances. Admittedly, these are generalisations but they reflect many of the issues that have led to the present sorry state of music resourcing in too many schools.

In view of this, it is essential that, as part of a subject development plan, particular emphasis is placed on producing a detailed, well-researched resource investment plan. Resources, in this context should include not only instruments, books, recordings, sheet music and software but also personnel and time. However, in this section, we will focus on equipment. Auditing of expertise and planning a cycle of staff development will be discussed in Chapter 16.

THE RESOURCE PLANNING CYCLE

The planning cycle will reflect the cycle for the subject plan as a whole, and should focus on the following questions (see Figure 12.1).

Resource audit

The first stage must be to identify precisely what equipment is already available in the school; where it is located; who uses it; and what state of repair it is in. A checklist like that illustrated in Table 12.3 could help with this process.

As a result of this exercise, it will be possible not only to establish what is available but also whether it is worth having and whether it is being put to regular use and employed appropriately.

Figure 12.1 Resource planning cycle

Table 12.3 Example of a checklist

Item	Location	State of repair			Suitable for			Available to		
		VG	Satis	Unsat	YR	Y1	Y2	YR	Y1	Y2

Identification of need

The next stage is to determine what ideally the school should have in terms of resources. A suggested list of resources is included at the end of this book in order to help coordinators with this process.

Identifying costs

The full cost of providing the recommended equipment for each class will be vast but it needs to be identified, since it will give the senior management and governors a realistic assessment of what is required. Any existing equipment in an appropriate state of repair will, of course, need to be deducted from the list.

Identifying priorities

The school will now be in a position to decide on its priorities. It is surprising how often, in the past, schools with limited finances have chosen to invest in large numbers of the same item. A better policy would be to purchase individual examples of a wide range of instruments. Children can then be given turns in the use of such equipment, so that each child eventually has a wide range of experiences.

Drawing up a schedule of investment

Once the priorities have been established, the school can draw up a timed schedule of investment. One format that could help with this is given in Table 12.4.

Table 12.4 Example of a timed schedule of investment

Item	Cost	Cycle of purchase					Year groups to benefit			
		97–8	98–9	99–2000	01–02	02–03	Nursery	YR	Y1	Y2

It will be clear from such information precisely what the resource situation is at any particular moment and how the school intends to develop its resources in the current financial year and in the future. The initial process of conducting the resource audit and drawing up a plan can be quite cumbersome but, from then on, it becomes far easier, particularly if the information is held on disc, so that it can be updated quickly. This process will ensure that more efficient use is made of existing resources and that further investment is coherent and logical and makes best use of the money available.

Chapter 13

Devising a policy and scheme of work for music

THE SCHOOL MUSIC POLICY

Every maintained school is required by law to produce a prospectus, giving information on a range of specified issues, including the curriculum. In addition, schools are encouraged to produce a policy statement for each subject area. The advantage of a policy statement is that it

- supplements the information in the prospectus and provides more details of what is to be covered within a subject and how this is to be done;
- provides a means of relating the aims for a specific subject to those of other subjects and to the aims and mission statement of the school as a whole;
- informs new staff and reminds existing staff of the approach to be taken to the subject;
- provides a focus for a critical examination by governors, staff and other interested parties of the priorities for presentation and development within that subject – a very necessary requirement in music, where curriculum planning has too often been based on traditions and assumptions which have not been examined critically.

A policy, therefore, is a manifesto; it presents an overview of the general principles underlying the school's approach to the subject. The more detailed information of how these principles are to be put into practice will be contained in the scheme of work. The policy statement should remain fairly constant and should not need to be altered as often as a scheme. Nevertheless, it should never become a tablet of stone and, like all documents, should be revised periodically to reflect developments and changes of emphasis in the thinking on the subject.

Given its purpose and the mixed audience for which it is intended, a policy

- should be fairly short;
- should not go into an undue amount of detail;

- should be written in a readable and easily understandable form, with any technical terminology or jargon being kept to a minimum.

In the case of music, we suggest that a policy statement should address the following issues

- the aims of the subject;
- the time to be allocated to it;
- staff responsibilities;
- teaching strategies to be adopted;
- planning and monitoring procedures;
- the extra-curricular aspects of the subject.

Figure 13.1 is an example of these principles being put into practice in the music policy for one infant school.

Figure 13.1 Example of a music policy

MUSIC POLICY STATEMENT

AIMS

The aims of music education at this school are to enable all pupils to:

- have experience of active involvement in music-making through performing, composing, improvising, listening and appraising;
- have access to music from a wide range of historical and cultural origins;
- have access to the music of female as well as male composers;
- develop skills in singing alone and in groups;
- develop skills in performing on tuned and untuned instruments;
- develop skills in performing in mixed instrumental and vocal groups;
- be able to identify and use the constituent elements of music;
- acquire an understanding and experience of using elementary notation techniques;
- develop basic musical vocabulary to enable them to discuss their own and others' works;

TIME ALLOCATION

Every pupil within the school will receive the equivalent of at least one hour's teaching in music per week. **In addition**, pupils will attend hymn practices.

OUTLINE OF THE ROLE OF THE MUSIC COORDINATOR

The music coordinator will:

continued . . .

- take the lead in policy development and the production of schemes of work designed to ensure progress and continuity in music throughout the school;
- support colleagues and give help, when required, in their implementation of the scheme;
- monitor progress in music and advise the headteacher on any action required;
- oversee the assessment of music and the procedures for reporting to parents on pupils' progress in this area of the curriculum;
- take responsibility for the purchase and organisation of central resources for music;
- keep up-to-date with developments in music education and brief colleagues as necessary;
- develop extra-curricular musical activities;
- identify staff developmental needs and arrange appropriate INSET.

OUTLINE OF THE ROLE OF THE CLASS TEACHER

It is the responsibility of every class teacher:

- to teach music, within the legal guidelines and the school's policy and scheme of work, to every child in her/his class;
- to record pupils' progress in the subject;
- to prepare reports to parents on pupils' progress;
- to seek advice and help where necessary from the music coordinator.

OUTLINE OF TEACHING STRATEGIES TO BE ADOPTED

All pupils will gain a variety of learning experiences through a combination of whole class work, group work and individual activities. Practical exploration of music will be central to all lessons in the subject.

PLANNING AND MONITORING

All teachers will:

- plan lessons from *Take Note* and *Silver Burdett*, in accordance with the sequence and time-scale indicated in the scheme of work;
- keep a record of work covered and adaptations which have to be made in the light of pupils' progress and other factors influencing school life;
- submit their records to the coordinator on a regular basis;
- make any necessary adaptations to their work in accordance with the advice given by the music coordinator.

continued . . .

MUSIC IN ASSEMBLY

- Music will be included in assembly to enhance the quality of the act of collective worship.
- This music will include listening to pieces of music as well as presentations of performances and compositions by the pupils.
- The music activity in assembly will be planned as an extension and development of National Curriculum requirements, particularly those relating to presenting music to others in a variety of contexts.

THE SCHEME OF WORK

Unlike the Policy Statement, the scheme of work will include far more detailed information and will need, where necessary, to address technical aspects of the subject. It should be written in way that will enable the head-teacher, teachers, governors, inspectors and any other interested parties to identify:

- precisely what is to be covered in the subject and when and how it is to be covered;
- the degree of continuity and progression in the pupils' experiences within the subject;
- how learning is to be monitored and assessed.

Every member of staff should be involved in devising the scheme. However, if the procedure is to be manageable, there is a need to define particular responsibilities. Precisely how this is done will vary between schools, depending on their nature, size and management styles.

Year group planning

Some schools favour planning in year groups, with all the teachers responsible for a particular age group deciding together on what is to be covered in a specific subject over a defined period of time. This has the advantage of ensuring continuity between classes of pupils of the same age but is not always effective in ensuring development from one year to another or continuity of experience across a key stage. In the worst instances, year group planning can result in three separate schools co-existing within one infant establishment.

Planning by the subject coordinator

Another approach is for the subject coordinator to plan the programme for the whole school, giving precise details of exactly what is to be taught by each teacher throughout the year. This enables progression to be matched with continuity. With the pressure of having to plan for ten subjects, more and more schools are seeing the advantages of adopting this approach across the whole curriculum. Some teachers, however, find this rather limiting.

Combination of the above approaches

A compromise is for the coordinator to establish the 'backbone' of the planning and for teachers within each year group then to add the detail, using material which they feel is appropriate to their particular classes.

The success of any approach will depend on a variety of factors. Size of the school has already been mentioned. The range of subject knowledge within the staff is another factor, as is the nature and quality of relationships within the school. But, whatever approach is taken, it is essential that:

- roles and expectations are clearly defined;
- teachers are clearly accountable for what they are doing;
- the curriculum is broad and balanced, and meets legal requirements;
- curriculum delivery ensures both progression and continuity in the pupils' experiences.

SEQUENCING THE PROCESS OF PRODUCING THE SCHEME OF WORK

The first stage in the production of the scheme of work is to determine what should be covered. Here the National Curriculum Documentation will be useful, but only to a certain extent. The original report of the Music Working Party was welcomed by primary teachers – music specialists and generalists alike – because of the detailed help it provided. The difficulty with the post-Dearing National Curriculum documentation is that it tells you where to travel to but does not give sufficient detail of what precise steps need to be taken to get there. As Pratt and Stephens (1995) have pointed out, there is a need to unpack the information and to elaborate on the programmes of study if they are to be at all helpful to teachers – particularly those with limited confidence or experience in the subject.

The need for identifying a developmental sequence for the elements of music

As was seen in Chapter 2, the elements of music form the central focus for this subject. Knowledge, skills and understanding in relation to these elements have to be developed through active involvement in composing and performing, listening and appraising. These activities should, wherever possible, be interrelated.

The logical way forward, therefore, is for a developmental sequence to be established for each musical element, progressing from the most basic response to the final expected response for the end of a specific key stage. When sequences have been established, there is then a need to present them in way that ensures:

• that each element is revisited periodically, to ensure consolidation and development of previous learning;
• that various elements are interrelated at appropriate levels of difficulty;
• that no element is emphasised at the expense of the others.

When this has been done, there is a need to identify appropriate sources of music and ideas to cover each stage. This will come from the examination of existing publications within the school and elsewhere. It is only when the developmental sequence for each element has been established and organised into periods of time that the scheme can be constructed.

Suggested developmental sequences for each musical element

The sequences below are presented as a guide and help to the reader. While they progress from the simplest to the most complicated activity, there is no reason why some activities could not be arranged in a different order. Given the different nature of classes, this will undoubtedly be necessary.

Duration

1 Maintaining beat/pulse while reciting nursery rhymes and simple poems.
   Movements produced while pupils sit/kneel.
   Body sounds and sounds in immediate environment used to mark beat.
2 Maintaining beat/pulse while singing nursery rhymes and simple songs.
   Movements produced while pupils sit/kneel.
   Body sounds and sounds in immediate environment used to mark beat.
3 As for 2, this time using range of movements suggested by the words of the songs for example, rocking movements, action of hammering/tapping, swaying, etc.
4 Accenting beats for example, patting and clapping, rowing movements, swinging movements, etc.
5 As for 3, this time to more complex songs.
6 Maintaining beat while moving round the room. Variety of movements for example, marching, skipping etc.

7   Accenting beats while involved in wider range of movements round the room for example, marching with one shoe off and one shoe on.
8   As for 6 and 7, this time with the addition of unpitched percussion instruments.
9   Echo clapping of rhythmic patterns of words.
10 Echo clapping of rhythms without words.
11 Transfer of 9 and 10 onto unpitched percussion instruments.
12 Use of 'human notes' for rhythmic patterns.
13 'Reading and writing' activities using 'human notation'.
14 Use of picture representations of rhythmic patterns.
15 'Reading and writing' activities using picture representations.

Pitch

1   Learning rhymes which focus on spatial concepts of 'high' and 'low'. Reinforcement of spatial concepts through movement.
2   Singing songs involving the concepts of 'high', 'low', 'up', 'down'. Spatial concepts reinforced via appropriate movements.
3   Movement Games where children make high or low shapes in response to high or low sounds.
4   As for 3, this time with children responding through physical movement to melodic progressions 'up' or 'down'.
5   Pitch 'writing' games. Children make high/low, up/down movements which have to be converted into pitches on chimebars and other pitched percussion instruments.
6   As for 3, this time with the children responding to 'high', 'low' and 'in the middle' sounds.
7   'Reading' and 'writing' activities using body shapes to indicate pitch.
8   All activities 3 to 8 extended through addition of further notes, necessitating more subtle response on the part of the pupils.

Timbre (tone colour)

1   Experimenting with sounds made by individual instruments.
2   Identifying names and pictures of instruments.
3   Classifying instruments according to way they are made, for example wooden, metal, skin, etc.
4   Discussing the nature of the sounds made, for example tinkling, clanging sounds, etc.
5   Classifying groups of instruments on basis of sounds made.
6   Identifying instruments from sound alone.
7   Matching pictures of instruments to sounds heard.
8   Matching names of instruments to sounds heard.

9   Playing 'Snap!' games based on matching names, pictures and names, pictures names and words.
10 Children, in pairs or in two groups, match instruments on basis of sounds heard.
11 Finding how many different sounds can be made on one instrument.
12 Identifying, by listening alone, how a sound has been made on a specific instrument.

Pace

1   Discussing speeds of movement of objects encountered in every day life.
2   Discussing the sound effects of objects moving at different speeds.
3   Moving to a beat which goes quickly or slowly.
4   Moving to a beat which gets faster.
5   Moving to a beat which gets slower.
6   Adjusting the weight on the metronome to make it move faster or slower.
7   Listening to pieces of music to determine whether they move quickly or slowly.
8   Responding with varying movements to sound clues which are fast or slow.
9   Singing songs and moving quickly or slowly as words dictate.
10 As for 9 but this time increasing or decreasing speed.
11 Improvising instrumental pieces which move at different speeds.

Dynamics

1   Experimenting with every day objects and helping the children anticipate whether the sounds they produce will be loud or soft.
2   Listening for loud and soft sounds in the world around us.
3   Listening for loud and soft sounds in pieces of music played.
4   Using loud and soft sounds as clues for hunting the thimble.
5   Performing echo songs.
6   Listening for echoes in pieces of music heard.
7   Producing loud and soft sounds on the same instrument and using these to improvise and compose.
8   Producing loud and soft sounds on a series of instruments and using these to improvise and compose.
9   Singing contrasting songs using loud and soft sounds.
10 Singing contrasts of volume within the same song.
11 Listening to changes of volume in pieces of music and discussing the effects which the composer produces by changing the volume.

Structure

1 Performing songs which have repeated patterns. Drawing the children's attention to this through discussion.
2 Listening for repeated patterns in pieces of music being performed.
3 Singing verse and chorus songs and drawing attention to similarities in shape.
4 Singing call and response songs.
5 Using repeated patterns to give shape to improvisations and compositions.

Texture

1 Playing individual instruments and combinations of instruments. Listening to and discussing the effects of this with the children.
2 Games of identifying whether one instrument or more than one is playing. (This can later be extended to determining which instruments are being played).
3 Listening to compositions involving individual instruments and combinations of instruments.
4 Performing simple rounds.

Finding ideas to help teach the elements

Once the sequence of possible activities has been established, the next step is to trawl through books and other materials, including those which teachers have created themselves, to see how, where and when the various ideas can be best used. This is an important way of involving the whole staff and recognising the contributions that all can make to the planning process. Through this process an 'ideas bank' can be established that relates to each element and each stage in the development of the children's grasp of that element.

Table 13.1 is an example of an 'ideas bank' for sections of the timbre sequence. Further details of the books listed in this chart are included in the resource lists at the end of this book.

Sequencing the activities into a defined time-scale

The next stage is to decide how to arrange the activities into a defined time-scale. The SCAA publication, 'Planning the Curriculum at Key Stages 1 and 2' (1995), describes ways of planning the curriculum based on units of work: 'Continuing Work' and 'Blocked Work'.

'Continuing Work' requires regular teaching; a progressive sequence of learning objectives; time for the systematic and gradual acquisition,

Table 13.1 An 'ideas bank' for teaching sections of the timbre sequence

Timbre (tone colour)

1 Experimenting with sounds made by individual instruments.	*Musical Starting Points With Young Children* pp.96–98 *Adventures in Music for the Very Young* pp.11–13 *The Music Box Songbook* p.12 and 69
2 Identifying names and pictures of instruments.	*Silver Burdett Book 1* p.57
3 Classifying instruments according to way they are made for example, wooden, metal, skin etc.	*Music Connections* p.35 and 37
4 Discussing the nature of the sounds made for example, tinkling, clanging sounds etc.	*Musical Growth in the Elementary School* pp.50–51
5 Classifying groups of instruments on basis of sounds made.	*Silver Burdett Book 1* pp.202–209 *Music Connections* pp.36 and 37
6 Identifying instruments from sound alone.	*Music Play* pp.106–107 and 227 *Music With Mr Plinkerton* p.37 *Blueprints Music Key Stage 1* p.21 *Music Connections* p.33
7 Matching pictures of instruments to sounds heard.	*Adventures in Music for the Very Young* p.31
8 Matching names of instruments to sounds heard.	*Blueprints Music Key Stage 1* pp.39–40
9 Playing 'Snap!' games based on matching names, pictures and names, pictures, names and words.	*Blueprints Music Key Stage 1* p.39
10 Children in pairs or in two groups match instruments on basis of sounds heard.	*Blueprints Music Key Stage 1* p.40
11 Finding how many different sounds can be made on one instrument.	*Music Connections* p.14 and 34 *Targeting Music Year 1* p.18
12 Identifying by listening alone how a sound has been made on a specific instrument.	*The Music Box Songbook* p.118

practice and consolidation of skills, knowledge and understanding. 'Blocked Work', on the other hand, is drawn from a single subject or curricular area which can be taught within a defined time of a term or less. It focuses on a distinctive and cohesive body of knowledge, understanding and skills, and can be taught alone or linked to other aspects of the curriculum. Given the nature of music and the need to develop skills through constant repetition and revisiting, we would argue that planning it on the basis of 'Continuing Work' would be most advisable and this is the approach used in Table 13.2.

In Table 13.2, the coordinator has chosen a 'spiral' approach, so that the children revisit concepts at regular intervals and pursue the activities in greater depth each time. She has also ensured that children are introduced to more than one concept at a time. The numbers relate to the numbers in the developmental sequences on pp. 223–226. Thus Duration 1 =

- Maintaining beat/pulse while reciting nursery rhymes and simple poems.
- Movements produced while pupils sit/kneel.
- Body sounds and sounds in immediate environment used to mark beat.

The teacher has deliberately planned for fewer weeks than there normally are in a school year, in order to allow for slippage through illness and other unexpected circumstances and for the possibility of more time than planned having to be spent on some activities.

Having decided on the time allocation for each element, and how far to progress within each term and over the year, the coordinator can now draw on the 'ideas banks' to produce a more detailed plan. The advantage of this approach is that it presents a clear map of how each element is to be addressed and how development is to be ensured across the term, the year and the Key Stage. It also allows for a range of disparate source materials to be welded together into a coherent scheme, tailored to the needs of the particular school.

ADAPTING COMMERCIAL SCHEMES TO THE SCHOOL'S OWN SCHEME

Rather than drawing on a range of source materials, many schools have invested in commercial schemes. The criticism often levelled at them in such circumstances is that they rely too heavily on the commercial materials and do not adapt them sufficiently to their own particular circumstances. However, in a subject where staff often lack confidence, the use of commercial schemes can be very helpful. The best schemes also have a built in sense of continuity and development which helps makes the teacher's job easier.

Table 13.2 A possible time-scale for teaching concepts to a reception class

YR	Term 1	Term 2	Term 3
Week 1	Duration 1	Duration 1 & 2 Reviewed / Different songs and rhymes	Dynamics 4
Week 2		Pitch 1 & 2 High & Low	Pace 3
Week 3	Timbre 1	Duration 3	Pitch 2
Week 4			Pace 4
Week 5	Duration 2	Timbre 2	Pitch 3
Week 6		Pitch 1 & 2 Up & Down	Pace 5
Week 7			
Week 8	Pace 1 & 2	Dynamics 2	Timbre 4
Week 9	Dynamics 1		
Week 10	Dynamics 1 & Timbre 1	Timbre 3	Duration 4
Week 11		Dynamics 3	
Week 12	Christmas Preparation		Texture 1

Even so, they will need to be adapted to fit the specific circumstances of the school and the anticipated rate of progress of specific classes. In Table 13.3, the work is based entirely on one published scheme – the Silver Burdett Music Scheme. Some schools take one scheme as a core scheme and supplement it with further materials drawn from a parallel scheme which the school had also bought. Supplementary materials can be incorporated easily into the table as it stands or by means of an additional column.

The way in which the plan has been set out enables the reader to establish at a glance what is to be taught when, what activities and musical elements are to be covered, what the balance between activities is, when the pupils are to be assessed and when the extension materials in the scheme are to be used. This approach also identifies when the coordinator is required to provide assistance, for example by explaining a term or demonstrating an idea. This ensures focused and efficient use of that person's time and efforts.

PLANNING FOR MIXED YEAR GROUPS

The above plan is designed for schools where children are taught in separate year groups. Many small schools, however, are faced with the problem of having to plan for more than one year group within the same set of lessons. There are three basic approaches that can be used to deal with this situation.

Approach 1

The first strategy is to produce separate plans for each year group and to arrange the timetable so that each age group is taught music at a different time. This has the advantage of helping to ensure that there is development in the work pursued by each child and that each child is appropriately challenged. The disadvantage is the amount of time that this takes. If the same strategy were adopted for all curricular areas the length of the school week would have to be doubled. However, because the subject matter of other curricular areas does not exist in time in the way that music does, there is no need for this. It is common practice, for example, for children of different levels of ability to pursue activities in the core subjects simultaneously. The time saved in this way then makes room for the extra allocation for music and there are some schools who use this strategy to good effect.

Approach 2

A second strategy is to choose materials that are appropriately differentiated and can be taught to pupils of a range of abilities simultaneously.

Table 13.3 A possible approach to presenting *Silver Burdett Music* to a reception class

Term 1

Week	Page	Listen	Perform	Compose	Extend	Elements	Coord.	Diff.	Assm.
1	6	•	•			rhythm	•		
2	7		•	•		rhythm	•		
3	8	•	•	•		t. colour	•		
4	11	•	•			rhythm			
5	9	•	•	•		t.colour			
6	16		•	•		melody			
7	12	•	•			rhythm			
8	13		•	•		rhythm			
9	14		•			rhythm			
10	15		•			form	•	•	
11	18	•	•			melody			

Term 2

Week	Page	Listen	Perform	Compose	Extend	Elements	Coord.	Diff.	Assm.
1	20		•	•	•	t.colour			
2	22	•	•	•		form	•	•	
3	23		•	•		rhythm	•	•	
4	24		•			rhythm			
5	26	•	•	•		melody & t.colour			
6	27	•	•		•	t.colour			
7	28		•			t.colour & express. qualities			
8	29	•	•	•		rhythm	•	•	
9 & 10	30		•	•	•	melody, form & express. qualities			
11	32		•			express. qualities			

Term 3

Week	Page	Listen	Perform	Compose	Extend	Elements	Coord.	Diff.	Assm.
1 & 2	42	•	•	•	•	t.colour & express. qualities	•		
3	44		•			form & express. qualities	•		
4	46		•	•		rhythm			
5	47		•			rhythm			
6	34	•				melody			
7	48	•	•			rhythm			
8	50		•	•		melody			
9	59					rhythm			
10 & 11	52 & 53					rhythm	•		•

Page references: Silver Burdett, Book 1

The problem here is finding such materials, especially if teachers do not have the time, or feel confident in their skills to make the appropriate adaptations themselves. Materials such as *Silver Burdett, Sounds of Music, Targeting Music* and *Blueprints: Music*, which have 'extension' sections added to basic lessons, can be useful in overcoming the problem.

Approach 3

A third strategy is to plan parallel activities over a two or three year cycle, depending on how many year groups are taught together. In this way, a child might encounter the same type of activity on two successive years but the content will be different.

Tables 13.4 and 13.5 give an example of work planned for a mixed class of Y1 and Y2 pupils. A child entering in Year 1 in one year will start with Plan A and go on to Plan B. A child entering Year 1 in the following year will start with Plan B and go on to Plan A. Obviously, to ensure progression, there will be a need to make greater demands on the older pupils who are revisiting a concept or activity and this will have to be highlighted in the short-term plan. In the tables, only the first term of each year is given. Similar arrangements would apply to the remaining two terms in each case.

PLANNING THROUGH TOPICS

Traditionally, there has been considerable emphasis in primary schools on teaching through topics and, at one time, it was difficult to envisage or find maintained primary schools adopting any other approach. With the arrival of the National Curriculum, however, there has been a considerable change. Many schools have moved to teaching subjects directly. Others have chosen to use a series of mini-topics for a particular age group. These topics vary in length, from a few weeks to half a term, to a full term. Other schools group some subjects into topics for part of the time, while teaching others as discrete bodies of knowledge.

The advantage of topic work is that it can help children to make connections between various areas of experience. Too often, teaching subjects separately can prevent or discourage individuals from trying to create an integrated overview of experiences (Phenix 1964). Topic work that is well-presented can also help motivate children (Dearden 1976). SCAA (1995) presents three circumstances in which linking work can be advantageous:

- when units contain common or complementary knowledge, skills and understanding;
- when skills acquired in one subject can be applied or consolidated in another context;
- the work in one curricular area provides a useful stimulus for work in another.

Table 13.4 A possible approach to presenting *Silver Burdett Music* to a mixed-age class YR–Y1: Term 1 Plan A

Week	Page	Listen	Perform	Compose	Extend	Elements	Coord.	Diff.
1	4		•		•	rhythm		
2	62	•	•	•	•	rhythm	•	•
3	7		•		•	rhythm	•	•
4	12	•	•	•	•	rhythm		
5	66		•		•	rhythm	•	•
6	8	•	•	•	•	tone colour		
7	56	•	•	•	•	tone colour		
8	59		•	•	•	tone colour		
9	16			•		melody		
10–11	112		•	•	•	expressive qualities		

Page references: *Silver Burdett, Book 1*

Table 13.5 A possible approach to presenting *Silver Burdett Music* to a mixed-age class YR–Y1: Term 1 Plan B

Week	Page	Listen	Perform	Compose	Extend	Elements	Coord.	Diff.
1	6	•	•		•	rhythm	•	
2	64	•	•	•	•	rhythm		•
3	10		•		•	rhythm		
4	13	•	•	•	•	rhythm		
5	65		•		•	rhythm		
6	9	•	•	•		tone colour		
7	58	•	•	•	•	tone colour	•	•
8	20		•	•		tone colour	•	•
						expressive qualities		
9	18		•	•		melody	•	
10	134				•	melody		
11	40	•	•			rhythm	•	•

Page references: *Silver Burdett, Book 1*

There are, however, disadvantages to an integrated topic approach. Given the considerable efforts that have been made by epistemologists to identify the uniqueness of 'forms of knowledge', 'realms of meaning' or 'modes of understanding' and to identify sequences of development within these areas, it can seem rather perverse to throw the whole lot back into one pot. It is certainly very time-consuming to construct an effective curriculum on this basis and, as Hirst and Peters (1970) have indicated, integrated approaches make considerable demands on teachers' knowledge and abilities.

Dearden (1976) has warned of the need for careful monitoring of integrated work to ensure that there is balance in what is presented over time, and that some subjects do not become under-represented. This is particularly important in music. Too often, it becomes an afterthought within a topic, with a song being included simply because the words are appropriate, with no consideration being given to its suitability in terms of range, the intervals used, its rhythmic patterns or how it contributes to children's musical growth. There is also a danger of the activities being sequenced in terms of what is suitable to the topic, at the expense of any logical development of musical skills or concepts. The topic approach is useful if it is used as a means to an end. Unfortunately it has too often become an end in itself.

If a topic approach is to be used, it is important:

- to identify precisely which subjects are going to contribute to the topic;
- to identify precisely what musical knowledge, skills and understanding are to be developed through the topic;
- to ensure that such knowledge, skills and understanding develop logically from pupils' previous learning in these areas;
- to ensure that the sequence of presentation of knowledge, skills and understanding during the course of the topic is designed to foster further development and help the children progress.

EXAMPLE OF A TERM'S WORK IN MUSIC BEING PLANNED AS PART OF A SERIES OF TOPICS

In Table 13.6, the teacher has planned music as part of an overall topic on Holidays but has done this in a way which recognises the individuality of music as part of the whole and in a way which will foster development of defined concepts through a combination of performance, listening and composition activities. She has also related the work pursued in class to the songs to be sung in assembly.

As well as collating materials from several sources, as this teacher has done, there are also several useful commercial schemes that make considerable use of topic work: *Sounds of Music* (Stanley Thornes), *Carousel* (Ginn), *Music Connections* (Cramer Music) and *Sounds Topical* (OUP).

Table 13.6 Example of music planned as part of a series of topics

Year: 1	Half term: 6		Topic: holidays
Lesson	Content	Reference	Elements
LITTLE CRAB	Listening activity and performing of song	*Silver Burdett*, p.70, Tape 3A-13-14-15, Keyboard or pitched percussion	Pitch and melody
STAMPING LAND	Performing of the song and adding accompaniment Movement game	*Silver Burdett*, p.80 Tape 3B-11, Chart 17, Musicling 6	Dynamics, tempo, rhythm
SEASIDE CHORUS 1	Performing rhyme 'Five Little Shells' Graphic representation	*Sing a Song 2*, Songs 1–3	Tone colour
SEASIDE CHORUS 2	Developing ensemble work Notation	*Bright Ideas: Responses to Music*, p.47	Dynamics Pitch
SEASIDE CHORUS 3	As above with the addition of ostinato	*Bright Ideas: Responses to Music*, p.48	Dynamics Pitch
MAN FROM THE SEA	Listen to various sea shanties	*Bright Ideas: Responses to Music*, pp.60–61	Dynamics Pitch
ASSEMBLY REPERTOIRE from *Rejoice* *Festivals*	*Hooray for Holidays*, p.92 *A Little Sandy Girl*, p.176		

LONG, MEDIUM AND SHORT-TERM PLANS

All the examples in this chapter so far have focused on long and medium term planning, since they indicate what is to be covered each year, term or week. From these, the short-term plan will need to be developed. The short-term plan should

- give details of how the work is to be presented;
- what differentiation strategies are to be used;
- how the work is to be assessed;
- what work will need to be revisited or re-emphasised in the light of previous assessment.

The precise format for short-term plans tends to vary considerably from school to school. In the case of the most detailed commercial schemes, teachers are presented with almost ready-made lessons that can be easily adapted to the school's own format.

If a school produces its own materials, rather than those available commercially, then more detail will be required in the lesson plan. If each class teacher had to produce a lesson plan for each of the subjects of the National Curriculum, the amount of work could become considerable. One way of avoiding this is to share responsibility for the planning. For example, in a three-form entry school, each teacher could take responsibly for preparing lesson plans for three or four subjects. They could then share these plans with each other, so that each teacher had a full set of plans. If this or some similar strategy is not adopted, the short-term planning is likely to become so superficial as to be meaningless. Another strategy to reduce effort is to word process each short-term plan and save it on disc. It will then be readily available for use on later occasions and can be very quickly adapted if needs be.

Figures 13.2 and 13.3 are two examples of short-term plans. In the first example there is a considerable amount of detail, reflecting the way that the lesson has been devised by the music coordinator. In Figure 13.3, because the commercial materials used already includes considerable detail on goals, organisation and materials, the information is less detailed.

The ideas presented here are by no means exhaustive or definitive. We present them simply as examples which have worked in various schools and which can be used by the reader as a spring board for further thought and discussion. Whether or not these or other approaches are adopted one thing is certain, it is essential that all work in music is structured into clear plans. As Salaman (1983) has warned, 'the alternative to structure in music education is not anarchy or total disaster or any other headline-making state of affairs; it is simply inefficiency.'

LESSON PLAN

Aims of Lesson
- To reinforce the notion of high and low and up and down, by matching appropriate movements to words during the performance of *Teddy Bear, Teddy Bear*.
- To enable children to convert pitch signs into sounds and vice versa.
- To give children further practice in moving in time to the underlying beat of the music.
- To develop accuracy of pitching and enunciation.
- To introduce the convention of reading notation from left to right.

Resources
Space for movement   Copymaster 59 from 'Blueprints Music'
Chimebars G and C   Further low and high pitched chimebars

continued . . .

Presentation   WHOLE CLASS ACTIVITY
1 Teacher presents song and movements.
2 Pupils reproduce movements while listening to the song on tape.
3 Pupils sing song without movements.
4 Pupils sing song with movements.
5 Individual pupils sing single verses while rest of the class perform actions.
6 Whole class performs song to chimebar accompaniment provided by the teacher.
7 More able pupils take turns in performing chimebar accompaniment while rest of the class sing and clap.
8 Teacher reminds class of high and low activity from previous lesson. Activity repeated, focusing on those children who experienced difficulty with this in the last lesson.
9 Game: The children sit in a circle. One child is blindfolded in the middle. The blindfolded child calls out the name of another child. The latter then reaches up high or goes down low. The teacher plays a high or low chimebar accordingly. On the basis of the sound, the blindfolded child has to decide what type of movement has been made. Chimebars both on table for this activity.
10 One child is at the chimebars. The other children stand in line and make high or low gestures. The teacher walks behind the children from left to right (as viewed by the chimebar player). As she does so she points to each child in turn. The chimebar player then plays the appropriate pitch to match the gesture being made.
11 As an *extension* of this, the children will play the same game, this time using the Teddy Bear cards. It is anticipated that some children will find difficulty reading from left to right while playing in the other direction. Therefore there will be a need to focus further on this activity in the next lesson.

Differentiation
During the *whole class* activity, more able pupils will be given greater challenge by being asked to play the chimebar accompaniment, while the less able pupils will receive particular attention when re-visiting high and low activities from the previous lesson.

Success Criteria
Pupils being able to:

• sing confidently and accurately;
• maintain ensemble when singing and playing together;
• differentiate between high and low sounds;
• able to maintain a beat;
• beginning to be able to convert signs into sounds and sounds into signs.

Figure 13.2 Example of a detailed music lesson plan

LESSON PLAN

Aims of Lesson
- To enable the children to explore and describe sounds.
- To enable them to choose sounds and control the elements of timbre and dynamics.
- To enable them to use these sounds to create a musical representation of a windy day.
- To give them the opportunity to discuss the way that a well known composer uses sounds to depict a storm.

Resources
Untuned instruments for shaking, scraping and striking.
Recording of Mussorgsky's *Night on a Bare Mountain*.

Sequence and Assessment
See *Targeting Music* (Dorothy Taylor) pp.18–19

Differentiation
Groups 1 and 2 will be given more oral prompts from the teacher to help them develop their general and musical vocabulary.
Group 3 and 4 will be expected to use appropriate musical vocabulary and to present their explanations and commentaries in more extended sentences.
Group 5 – as for 3 and 4 but they will also be given the opportunity to write down their responses in simple sentences either during the lesson or at a later point.

Figure 13.3 Example of a music plan based on commercial materials

Chapter 14

Monitoring delivery of the music curriculum

AN APPROACH TO SUCCESSFUL MONITORING

However detailed and beautifully presented a school's curriculum plans might be, they will be of no use whatsoever unless they are actually put into practice. Schools, therefore, need to set up monitoring procedures to ensure that this is happening. Too often, headteachers equate monitoring with releasing members of staff to observe each others' work or enabling a coordinator to demonstrate to others how a particular aspect of a subject can be taught. There is undoubtedly a place for such strategies. However, their effectiveness can be increased if they are put into a wider context. In order to do so, there is a need for a school to know precisely what is being delivered each week; where there is 'slippage' in delivery; where adaptations need to be made and how those adaptations can be accommodated, without upsetting the overall plan and reducing it to no more than a paper exercise, to be forgotten once the 'real' business of teaching begins. Below we describe one approach that has been used successfully by schools to monitor not only music but also other areas of the curriculum.

Stage 1: recording by individual members of staff

This involves each teacher completing the following form, shown in Table 14.1. Columns 1 and 2 are completed on the basis of the scheme of work and will be common to all teachers responsible for parallel classes in a particular year group. Column 3 will indicate what the teacher covered. This might correspond exactly with Column 2 or might differ from it. If in Week 3, for example, the teacher has only covered two of the three planned activities, he or she will have to decide how the remaining activity is to be accommodated. If it is decided to include it in a subsequent lesson, will the other activities have to be curtailed? If so, which ones are to be curtailed? Unless an adaptation of this type is made, the plan will spill over the time available for it. Rather than making these types of

Table 14.1 Form for recording delivery of music teaching

Year:			Term:	
Week	Planned work	Actual delivery	Adaptations made	Coordinator's comments

adaptation, the teacher might decide to omit the aspect which has not been covered, so that subsequent activities are given their due allowance of time.

At the other end of the spectrum, a teacher might find that he or she has covered the planned work in less time than was envisaged. In this case, decisions will have to be made about whether to introduce additional activities or bring subsequent work forward. Such adaptations will inevitably have to be made during the delivery of a scheme, otherwise it will become an inflexible end in itself, rather than a means to an end. The important thing is to ensure that the adaptations are recorded and their implications carefully examined.

Stage 2: examination of teachers' records by the coordinator or senior manager

Even when each teacher has considered and noted the adaptations to the scheme, there is a further problem to be faced. If each teacher within a year group does this in isolation, the situation will soon be reached where there is little comparability and continuity between what is presented to children in parallel classes. For this reason and also to ensure progression across the whole school, there is a need to review the records at regular intervals. Some schools choose to do this at the end of a term. However, this is too late, since it does not allow enough time for intervention if serious problems of omission have arisen. Therefore we would suggest that each teacher's record should be examined by the coordinator, or other member of the management team, at four-weekly intervals. In this way, further problems can be identified and allayed through the advice given in Column 5 of the form.

It could be argued that some teachers would resist such an approach and see it as a lack of trust in their abilities. However, if the same approach is being used for all subjects and if different people are responsible for different areas of the curriculum, everyone would be in a position of accounting for, and being accountable to a colleague, and the whole system would be seen to be fair. Ultimately, however, it is the fair treatment of the child that is paramount and no school should be without a means of identifying whether its pupils are receiving their curricular entitlement.

Another advantage of a regular review of records is that the coordinator is then in a position to take an overview of the subject, analyse the emerging patterns and to decide on appropriate action to improve the programme. Imagine, for example, that three teachers of Y2 classes have been teaching lessons that are meant to include performing and composing activities. Teacher A has covered all the work. Teachers B and C, however, have not delivered the composition aspect. The coordinator will have to consider the possible reasons for this situation. Do teachers B and C lack the skills or confidence to deliver the composition work? If so, this will have implications for the staff development programme. Is it that they have got carried away by the performance activities and have therefore not been able to deliver the composition activities, able though they both are to tackle them with the children? If so, there is an issue of timing to be considered. Is the lack of emphasis on composition a reflection of a lack of resources? After teacher A had helped herself to the few tuned instruments in the school, there might have been nothing left for the other two. Or could it be that teachers B and C have taken care over their work and produced high standards for their classes while Teacher A has kept so slavishly to the scheme that she has been content to accept sub-standard work from her pupils?

Stage 3: establishing strategies for improvement

The answers to such questions might be obvious on reflection, and the coordinator will be able to offer advice with confidence. It might be a decision to include composition activities in the next round of in-service training in music, either for the whole school or for specific members of staff. On the other hand, the situation might be far more difficult to decipher. In which case, the coordinator might decide to visit colleagues' classrooms to gain more information.

A visit of this type will have a clear purpose and, therefore, is likely to be a better use of time than some random release on a regular basis for half a term, in the pious hope that the main problems will conveniently come to light when it is the music coordinator's turn to be released.

The follow-up to such visits will also need to be carefully considered. Let us imagine that, after visiting teachers B and C, both of whom would say they are 'non-specialists', the coordinator decides that they would benefit from observing another at work. The coordinator herself might decide to conduct the demonstration work but her colleagues might decide that it is only because of her musical knowledge that the lesson has been successful. To overcome such 'avoidance techniques', it might be better for the coordinator to use any time made available to release Teacher A who, despite being a 'non-specialist', has managed to conduct the composition work successfully. This might be a far better way of boosting the other colleagues' confidence.

Stage 4: reporting to the headteacher and governors

As a result of the regular review of records and/or visits to classrooms, the coordinator will be well placed to provide the headteacher with a more informed picture of the strengths and weaknesses of music delivery within the school. This information can, in turn, be relayed to the governors who are ultimately legally responsible for the delivery of the curriculum. It can also provide them with hard evidence in relation to in-service training and resource needs for the subject and help them to make better informed decisions on financing the curriculum.

Stage 5: modifying the scheme of work

If the required changes to the scheme have been recorded on a regular basis throughout the year, the school will be able to establish what has actually been delivered, as opposed to what was planned, and to identify areas of mismatch. This information can then be collated to help refine the plan for the following year. In this way, the scheme should improve from year to year. If the information is word processed, all that will be required, once the initial plan has been set up, is a simple cutting and pasting process, rather than the unwieldy, energy-sapping, time-wasting, soul-destroying activity that any adaptation to the curriculum too often brings in its wake.

Chapter 15

Assessment, recording and reporting

WHY SHOULD WE ASSESS?

Assessment is an essential part of the teaching and learning process. It helps us to establish what children have learnt and in what areas they need further help. This can apply to learning in one lesson, in a series of lessons, or over a key stage. In this way, the attainment and progress of individuals or a class can be determined. On the basis of the information gathered, we can judge how successful our teaching has been and what aspects of it need to be reinforced or altered. Such alterations might consist of modifying the format and content of specific lessons or making adaptations to the overall scheme. It might lead to the regrouping of children or to changes in the resources used.

TYPES OF ASSESSMENT

There are two types of assessment: formative and summative. Formative assessment helps us to establish the effectiveness of teaching and learning in a specific lesson or a defined series of lessons. Summative assessment establishes levels of achievement at key points during the education process, such as the end of key stages.

On the basis of a summative assessment, we can compare the attainment and progress of individual children with that of other children in the same school, in neighbouring schools or in the country as a whole. In addition, it enables us to compare the performance of successive groups of children over time, either within one institution or across the country. Some of this information will be of immediate concern to the individual teacher, while other aspects of it will be of particular interest to those responsible for determining policy, either within a school or on a wider front, locally and nationally.

Summative assessments in core subjects take the form of statutory externally-set tests (SATs) at the end of each key stage. In the case of the foundation subjects, a summative assessment is made by the teacher against a series of End of Key Stage Descriptions (EKSDs). In most core subjects, the EKSDs enable the teacher to identify several levels of attainment. In the case of music, however, there is only one EKSD for each key stage.

WHAT CANNOT BE ASSESSED?

It is important to recognise that, however detailed the criteria that we use and however effective the assessment procedures we use might be, there are aspects of children's development which will be well nigh impossible to assess. Pratt and Stephens (1995), for example, point out that simply because 'a child might not have developed the vocabulary to express an emotional or aesthetic response does not mean that the response does not take place'. Similarly, Swanwick (1988) points to the impossibility of devising a test which can assess the ability of E. M. Forster as a novelist or Rembrandt as a painter. In view of this, Swanwick suggests that assessment in the arts might be considered an extension of teaching.

ADVANTAGES AND DISADVANTAGES OF TEACHER-BASED ASSESSMENT

The fact that assessment in music is teacher-based has been welcomed by some because it allows it to be more closely integrated into the teaching process. However, there are also disadvantages to this arrangement. Because the EKSDs for music are so limited, it is difficult to give a detailed statement of attainment or to differentiate between levels of attainment. The lack of specificity in the assessment criteria also makes it difficult to ensure comparability between the assessments made by several members of staff within a school or across several schools. Therefore, both their validity and reliability are questionable. This, in turn, makes it very difficult to gain an accurate picture of pupils' musical attainment nationally or locally, or to draw any meaningful comparisons.

One way of overcoming the problem of lack of detail, according to Pratt and Stephens (1995), is to revive the levels defined in the first draft of the Music National Curriculum Order. The disadvantage is that those levels are no longer readily available to most teachers. The problem of lack of consistency and comparability between teacher assessments has been addressed by the School Curriculum and Assessment Authority (SCAA) in *Consistency in Teacher Assessment* (SCAA 1995) which will be discussed later in this chapter.

However, there is one major difficulty with teacher assessment in music that has received little attention. As we saw in Chapter 11, primary teachers tend to lack confidence in music and have therefore traditionally avoided teaching it. The immediate concern for many of them, therefore, is to pluck up enough courage to tackle the subject. The lack of external assessment helps this process to a certain extent. But there is a further problem highlighted by the following questions which primary teachers ask time and time again: 'How can someone who is only just beginning to dare to teach a subject be expected to have the confidence to assess pupils' progress in it? How will they know what to look and listen for?'

One way of overcoming this problem, in the short term, might be to make assessment – particularly summative assessment – the main responsibility of the music coordinator who could guide the teacher. In many instances, however, the coordinators themselves need help. Another solution might be for schools in a neighbourhood to share the expertise of a member of staff who could be used to oversee assessment. The disadvantage of this, of course, is the cost in money, time and the disruption to classes. An alternative would be for music support services to train staff in this area and sell the services to schools at particular times of the year. Whatever approach is taken to the management and administration of assessment, there are certain principles which should be central to it.

BASIC PRINCIPLES OF ASSESSMENT

A review of some of the literature on this subject (for example, Taylor 1986, Durrant and Welch 1995, Pratt and Stephens 1995) highlights certain basic principles which should be reflected in any assessment of children's musical development.

Assessment should:

- be an integral part of planning and be designed to reflect, rather than to determine, what is taught;
- be manageable, in terms of the mechanisms and time involved;
- be an integral part of classroom activity;
- draw on a wide range of evidence;
- be appropriate to the task;
- involve pupils themselves in reflecting on their own work;
- focus on process as well as product.

PRINCIPLES IN PRACTICE

Assessment as an integral part of planning

In planning, we need to ask a series of questions

- What do we want the children to learn? (Aims)
- How can they best be helped to learn this? (Teaching and learning processes)

Only then should we ask in what ways we can assess how effectively the children have learnt. In this way we can help ensure that the assessment is a means to an end and not an end in itself. We certainly should not be asking what it is feasible or possible to assess and then teach towards the assessment.

Managing the assessment

The scheduling of the assessment will depend on the type of information and degree of detail which we want to discover. Some types of information can be gleaned more readily from one kind of activity than from another. Some information will give a general picture of the progress and attainment of a class as a whole. Other information will relate more specifically to individuals. In both cases, the information will contribute to an evaluation of the effectiveness of the overall programme.

General information

General information will focus on the broad picture of attainment, progress and response in a lesson or series of lessons. It will consist of asking the following types of questions:

- Attainment
  How many children are able to perform a particular task accurately?
  What are the general patterns of understanding or misunderstanding in the class?
- Progress
  How much of the planned work has been covered in the time allowed for it?
  How long has it taken the class to grasp the skill or concept?
  How much have the children remembered or forgotten from previous lessons?
- Response
  How much enthusiasm for the work is there among the children?
  What is the general level of concentration in the class?

The answers to these questions might not be formalised, but reflecting on them will determine how we proceed with a lesson or series of lessons and what adaptations we have to make. These are the types of questions which experienced teachers ask themselves almost unconsciously, just as experienced drivers adapt their actions in relation to a plethora of information about a car's position, speed progress, state of the road, and so on. However, there is a need for formalised reflection at times, so that the information can be shared by staff. Writing down and reflecting on the pooled responses will help build a more detailed picture of the effectiveness of teaching and learning in a particular term, year or across the whole school. In this way, it can be used for individual evaluation by teachers of their own performance and general evaluation by the whole school of its effectiveness.

More specific information

However much general information a teacher might have about a class, what parents want to know is how their own child is progressing and what he or she can and cannot do. This requires far more detailed and complicated information gathering. The scheduling of this process is helped if we differentiate between what might be called regular and irregular activities, and between activities which can be assessed in a whole class situation and those which require more specific attention to individuals.

Regular activities

In a well-devised scheme, each pupil should be regularly involved in singing, playing instruments, listening, composing and moving to music. A teacher, working regularly with a class and observing the children as they work, should be able to produce fairly accurate answers to such questions as the following in relation to whether individual children can:

- sing accurately?
- beat in time to music?
- manage to play unpitched percussion instruments?
- play and sing in time with other children?

This is part of the knowledge of children that is built up by class teachers as they work with them day in day out. Even teachers who only work with a class for some part of the week should be able to answer such questions fairly confidently. If there is any doubt, they could always check out their answers with more focused observation of a particular child working on some specific task.

Integrating assessment into classroom activities

To refine this process, a teacher might choose to divide the class into groups of five or six, pay particular attention to the performance of a different group each lesson and keep a very brief record. This should be done during the course of the activities and should not replace the teaching or be made into some highly formalised activity. It is important also to ensure that observation is not concentrated so much on a defined group that a significant step in learning made by another child is ignored. In the same way, the teacher should not feel that the assessment of music should be confined to the music lesson. A child might display significant evidence of music attainment (being able to pitch or move in time to a beat, for example) in another context within class, or even in the playground. In the same way, a child might display a significant advance in the use of language while talking about a piece of music that he or she has heard or made. Here again, the class teacher has the advantage of working with the children over a series of activities and being in a position to observe such events.

Assessment approached in these ways – through general reflection and specific observation – fulfils the principles of manageability, appropriateness and integration highlighted earlier.

Example 1: integrating the assessment of singing into a lesson

Fifteen 5–6 year olds have learnt to sing 'Little Miss Muffet' over a simple two-note chimebar accompaniment to it. They are now preparing to play a timbre recognition game based on the song. The teacher explains that Jessica will play the part of Miss Muffet. She has to stand in the middle of the circle, wearing a blindfold. At a sign from the teacher, one of the other children will pretend to be a spider and creep up behind Miss Muffet, singing the song while doing so. Miss Muffet's task is to listen very carefully to the singer and work out which one of her class mates is playing the part of the spider. If the singer has been correctly recognised, he or she assumes the part of Miss Muffet (or Little John Muffet) and the game continues.

In order to help them to recognise each others' voices, the teacher asks each child, in turn, to sing the song to the rest of the class. As they do so, she takes the opportunity to assess how accurately and confidently each child is singing and makes a note of this in the child's record. In this way, the process of assessment is precise, focused and capable of being recorded without in any way detracting from the flow of the lesson or turning it into a false, unmusical situation. In this case, the small number of children helps the process. However, there is no reason why, in the case of a larger class, the assessment could not be spread over more than one occasion with different groups playing the game at different points in the week.

Example 2: integrating the assessment of pitch discrimination into a lesson

On a different occasion, the same class is discussing high and low sounds. They have been told the fable about the competition between the birds to see which of them can fly the highest. The wren eventually wins because it rides on the back of the eagle. When the eagle gets too tired to fly any more, the wren takes off and quickly outstrips the height reached by the larger bird.

They now perform a rhyme about aeroplanes flying high above the hill and boatmen rowing on the river far below. As they speak the words, the children stretch up high or crouch down low on the floor.

While they are resting from their efforts, the teacher plays them two musical extracts. The first is a performance of 'Bailero' from Canteloube's *Songs of the Auvergne* and the second is a section from the album *Traurig aber wahr* by the German rock band *Herzer*. The children are helped to identify the contrast between the high and low voices in the two extracts.

When this has been done, the teacher takes two chimebars: one high, one low. As she plays the high sound, the children reach up high and, as she plays the low sound, the children make a low, crouching movement. When they have practised this, she asks the children to turn their backs towards her and to repeat the activity, this time relying on their hearing to determine which gestures to make. As they do so, she makes a note of which children can and cannot perform the task accurately and enters this on their record. She will use this information in a later lesson to help identify which children need further practice and which ones need to be extended further. Again assessment is taking place without the lesson being interrupted and as part of a musical experience for the children involved.

Drawing on a wide range of evidence

Children can demonstrate their knowledge skills and understanding in a variety of ways. Let us focus further on understanding the differences between high and low sounds. This could be demonstrated through:

- movement;
- responding to pictures;
- speech;
- writing;
- performing.

In Example 2 given above, children can demonstrate that they can differentiate between high sounds by making appropriate choices between high or low bodily movements. Alternatively, they could look at a series of high or low movements made by the teacher or represented in a series of pictures and match these to high and low pitched sounds. On another occasion, they might be asked to apply the terms 'high' or 'low' to the sounds that they hear or to demonstrate their understanding by drawing a circle round the appropriate word 'high' or 'low' on a worksheet as they listen to sections of music being played. For those who find difficulty reading or who have not yet developed the skill, appropriate pictures could be used instead of the words, for example, a picture of an aeroplane for 'high' and a picture of a submarine for 'low'. They could also respond to a visual, written or spoken cue by singing a high or low sound. Alternatively they could show understanding, through a combination of methods, during a composition activity, as in the following example.

Example 3: assessing understanding of pitch during a composition activity

A group of 6–7 year olds have been making a composition based on 'Hickory Dickory Dock'. They have played their composition to the teacher and are now sticking cut-out pictures of mice at various heights on the wall, in order to 'notate' their music. One little girl is unhappy. She feels that not enough has been made of the rising pitch as the mouse runs up the clock. It should go 'much much more higher' she says and as she does so, she gets up and stretches so high that her whole face and body becomes contorted. She also makes a high strangulated sound at the back of her throat. This child is demonstrating, through a whole range of techniques, what she is imagining in terms of the pitch of the sound.

Some activities might give better evidence of a particular child's understanding than other approaches. For example, it is often assumed that because children cannot sing a high or low note when asked to do so, that they cannot hear the differences. In fact, when asked to demonstrate their understanding through movement, it is quite clear that even so-called monotones can hear the differences. The reason that they cannot sing the notes is to do with lack of development of control of the vocal cords, shyness or reluctance, not their hearing.

It is clearly important, therefore, that the teacher draws on evidence from a variety of tasks when assessing a child over the course of a key stage.

Involving the children in reflecting on their own work

In Example 3 above, the children are discussing and reflecting on what they have produced in a composition activity. To do so they have to remember what they produced and what effect it created, and decide whether it could be improved. They then try out and perform alternative sounds. The same could be done by asking the children to listen to a recording of themselves singing or playing instruments, and getting them to comment on their own work. In doing so, not only are the children performing, composing and listening but they are also providing evidence of their abilities to appraise their own and others' work.

Focusing on process as well as product

Imagine two children playing with plasticine. One of them rolls it into a ball and puts it on the table. The second child rolls the plasticine into a long sausage, then squashes it together before making a cube shape with it.

Finally, after various other explorations of this sort, this child also produces a ball and puts it on the table. The final products might be almost identical but, everything being equal, the second child will have discovered far more about the potential of the plasticine. He or she will have had to make several decisions about how to tackle the task, will have had to convert these into actions and then reflected on the acceptability of a variety of products before arriving at the final object. In other words, the second child will have been involved in far more learning. Because of this, it is important that, in music, we assess the process that leads to the product as well as the product itself.

Assessment of process will focus on identifying:

- the range of possibilities that a child suggests, explores or discusses before choosing a particular course of action;
- the reasons that the child gives for rejecting or accepting a particular strategy;
- the skills, knowledge and understanding that are exhibited by the child as the decision-making process takes place.

This can be seen in operation in Example 4.

Example 4: encouraging the class to learn through exploring

A group of 6–7-year-olds has been involved in exploring the range of sounds that they can make with their hands and feet. They are now using these sounds to make a musical representation of warm, windy weather turning into stormy rain. In discussion with the teacher, they have decided that the sounds of a warm, windy day can best be represented by everyone rubbing the palms of their hands together. The teacher then asks them how they can give the impression of rain drops. Jimmy volunteers to demonstrate and produces very loud rapid sounds with his fingers on the desk top. The teacher takes the class back to the beginning of the activity and, at the point where the rain starts, all the children repeat Jimmy's actions and make a rain drop sound. 'Do you like this?' asks the teacher. Most say they do. 'Can you think of a different way of doing it?' she asks. Luke suggests using stamping feet. After the whole class has tried this, Emily suggests that they could do both. Sarah develops the idea further by suggesting that some children could stamp while others make the finger sounds.

They try this out. Then Alex suggests that they could produce these sounds one after the other and then have both the finger and stamping sounds together. The class seems to like this. But the teacher suggests that it could be made even better. She asks the children to think back to the last time they saw rain. 'Did it all start at the same time?' After some prompting, Nicholas remembers that the rain started slowly and then got quicker.

He demonstrates this with hand sounds. So the lesson progresses until the class has agreed on a version for the rain piece.

In this process, the children are displaying several aspects of their knowledge, skills and understanding which would not have been apparent simply from an examination of the finished product. Each child who demonstrates provides evidence of his or her skills in controlling parts of the body to produce an intended sound. Both Jimmy and Luke can think of alternative sounds, while Emily and Sarah go a step further and show an understanding of how to give a shape to their sounds by combining or sequencing them in particular ways. Alex displays similar understanding and is able to take the process further still. Nicholas does the same but, in doing so, also displays an understanding of concept of tempo.

As with the earlier forms of assessment, this evidence can be gathered in a variety of ways. In this particular case, the teacher works with the class and watches and listens very carefully to their responses. She then makes brief notes on the children after the end of the lesson.

Alternatively, she could use a technique that she employs in other lessons. There, she sets a composition task and divides the class into groups to perform it. While they are working, she observes the children and makes notes of their responses. Although she focuses on one group at a time, she keeps an eye and ear open for interesting or unexpected developments in other groups. She is involved in recording, but not to the exclusion of teaching. When she feels that a suggestion or question from her could help move the children forward, she intervenes. This is entirely appropriate. She is, after all, involved in teaching, not in scientific observation.

Assessing the process of learning could also be helped in certain instances by making a tape or video recording of the children in action and examining it later. This can become too cumbersome if done too frequently, although it could be useful in building up a portfolio of evidence in relation to the class as a whole, or in order to help establish greater comparability between assessments made by several members of staff.

Another technique, applicable to older children, is to ask them to reflect on what they have done, through discussion or by writing about it. This will ensure that, in addition to focusing on process, the assessment is:

- manageable;
- appropriate to the task;
- an integral part of classroom activity;
- a means of extending the range of evidence;
- a way of encouraging the children to reflect on their own work.

We warned earlier of the danger of treating assessment as if it were a totally dispassionate observation of child behaviour and of the danger of becoming blinkered in our observations and not giving value to the unexpected. It will be possible in some instances to attend to one skill, concept or parameter more than another. Thus, at a particular time, we might be observing how well a child can pitch notes, at another time how well he or she can move in time to the beat of a piece of music, and at another whether the child can hear a particular tune in a recorded arrangement. However, in Example 4 above, information is being gathered on children's development in several aspects. Composition work is particularly well suited to this because of its essentially open-ended nature. Not only does it provide opportunities to assess children's command of various concepts and skill; it also gives insight in the processes of selection, rejection and modification which the children apply in generating musical ideas; and their developing powers in appraising their own and each other's work. Furthermore, it provides evidence of their linguistic development, particularly their ability to make appropriate use of subject-specific terminology.

RECORDING

Teachers will need to record the evidence which they gather from assessment. Here again, however, it is important to ensure that the systems used are manageable and do not detract from the process of teaching. For this reason, we agree with Pratt and Stephens (1995) when they discourage the use of tick sheets in the classroom, although there might be a place for them occasionally as is shown in the observation of the compositional process described above. We suggest that the following basic procedures could be helpful.

Drawing up a schedule for assessment

- In the process of drawing up the scheme of work, the teacher identifies the points where summative assessment is to take place. This might consist of a formal report at the end of the year or the end of a key stage, or a process of drawing together a broad picture of a child's attainment, making particular use of the information that we build up from regular contact with the children.
- At the same time, the teacher could identify points during a term or year where the whole class could be assessed through a listening test, for example.
- The teacher could then draw up a schedule for particular observation of specific children working alone and/or in groups.

The assessments should not be too frequent. A plant will not grow if you keep pulling it up to see how much its roots have developed.

Recording the results of the assessments

The results of assessments could then be recorded on a profile for the child. The precise format for this will vary, depending on the particular policies of individual schools. We suggest that the most manageable is one which covers the progress of a child across a key stage and which does not demand too much information. Table 15.1 is an example which the reader might wish to use as a prompt for discussion and adaptation.

Here the elements of music provide the starting point. Children can demonstrate progression in knowledge, understanding and skills in relation to these through each of the parameters of Listening, Performing and Composing. At each stage, the extent to which they can identify or produce these elements can be gauged on a five-point scale ranging from Low (scored 1) to High (scored 5).

This form would be used across the key stage. Using the evidence-gathering techniques described above, the teacher would reflect on a child's progress and enter a tick appropriately, so that gradually a profile would be created for each child as he or she moved through the key stage. Comparison of this profile with the base-line assessment, completed with the parents when the child entered the school (see Chapter 3), would also allow for the extent of progress to be identified and would indicate any modifications that might need to be made to the scheme of work.

REPORTING AT THE END OF KEY STAGE 1

It is a legal requirement that at the end of each key stage, schools should report on the extent to which each pupil's attainment relates to the standards expected of children after they have been taught the relevant programme of study. The expectations in music match the level of demand in other subjects. At Key Stage 1, they are broadly equivalent to Level 2.

The 'types and range of performance that the majority of pupils should characteristically demonstrate' by the end of each stage are printed in the 'End of Key Stage Descriptions'. The Level Description for Key Stage 1 reads as follows:

Attainment Target 1: Performing and Composing
Pupils sing a variety of songs and play simple pieces and accompaniments with confidence and awareness of pulse. They explore, select and order sounds, making compositions that have a simple structure and make expressive use of some of the musical elements including dynamics and timbre.

Table 15.1 A child's musical profile, based on the results of assessments

Element	Listening					Performing					Composing				
	1	2	3	4	5	1	2	3	4	5	1	2	3	4	5
PITCH 1: High/Low Sounds															
Identifies															
Produces															
PITCH 2: Movement up/down															
Identifies															
Produces															
PITCH 3: Steps and leaps up/down															
Identifies															
Produces															
TIMBRE 1: Individual instruments/voices															
Identifies															
Produces															
TIMBRE 2: Several instruments/voices separately															
Identifies															
Produces															
TIMBRE 3: Several instruments/voices together															
Identifies															
Produces															
BEAT 1: Large movements to beats															
Identifies															
Produces															
BEAT 2: Refined movements to beats															
Identifies															
Produces															
BEAT 3: Combinations of movements to beats															
Identifies															
Produces															
ACCENT : Accenting through movement															
Identifies															
Produces															

Attainment Target 2 : Listening and Appraising
Pupils respond to short pieces of music, recognising repetition and changes within the musical elements. They listen attentively and describe and compare sounds and pieces of music using simple terms.

Below are examples of reports on four Year 2 pupils, using the end of key stage descriptions as a guide.

Nathan

Nathan has a good singing voice that he uses confidently when performing alone and with others. He can sing a variety of songs accurately and can play simple pieces and accompaniments with an awareness of pulse. He can select and order sounds to make simple compositions and provides good leadership for his fellow pupils. He can perform music with good gradation in volume. He can recognise repetitions and changes in the music played to him. He listens attentively and can comment on the pieces that he hears.

Deborah

Deborah has a good singing voice. She sings confidently when performing solos as well as in a group. She can sing a variety of songs accurately and with a developing sense of musicianship. She can explore and select sounds to make simple compositions and is able to comment on the particular features of the music that she hears.

Natalie

Natalie has a good sense of pulse and her voice is developing well. She makes a good contribution to group singing and is able to produce gradations of volume and speed. Her compositions are developing and she can respond to the particular features of the music played in class but her progress is sometimes hampered by a lack of concentration.

Edward

Edward has a very good voice and he performs a variety of songs with confidence. He has a very strong sense of rhythm and phrasing and can maintain a pulse very well. He has good ideas when composing and he is able to make relevant comments on the music that he hears.

The same criteria could also be used to report on progress during the key stage. The following are examples of reports on two pupils at the end of YR and Y1 respectively.

Thomas

Thomas's singing voice is developing and he has a fair sense of pitch. He has more difficulty maintaining a pulse but this should develop with practice. He listens with interest to the music performed in class. He is beginning to explore sounds and to arrange them into simple compositions.

Emily

Emily's singing voice is developing well. She is beginning to explore sounds and arrange them into simple compositions. She listens attentively and shows interest in the music played in class. Her sense of pulse is a little insecure but this will no doubt improve with further practice and experience.

The procedures and tools for assessment presented here are not intended to be viewed as definitive statements but as a spur to further thought and a means of helping schools reflect on their existing practice and to refine it further.

Chapter 16

Activities for school based in-service development

THE NEED FOR A LONG-TERM PLAN

Deficiencies in the music teaching within a school will rarely have arisen overnight. Therefore, it is unlikely that they will be rectified over night. Not all headteachers recognise this, however, and it is not uncommon to find heads who expect a day's in-service course or a few hours of consultancy to solve all their problems, with minimum expenditure on time and resources. A training programme, if it is to have more than a passing impact on the life of a school, has to be planned to extend over time and should be regularly followed up so that ideas and skills are reviewed, refreshed and developed. It must also meet the needs of the specific members of staff concerned and be directly related to the particular scheme of work, resources and circumstances within which the school operates. This is why school-based in-service is very important, although that might arise from, or be enriched through, training geared to a large number of schools.

There are several stages in the process of planning an in-service programme which are as applicable to music as to other areas of the curriculum.

CONDUCTING A SKILLS AUDIT

The first stage is to establish what expertise already exists within the school through a skills audit. This might take the form of a questionnaire or a discussion forum.

It is not unusual, in these circumstances, to find more lights being hidden under bushels than might be expected. This is not always a case of teachers trying to avoid using their skills. It can result from an underestimation of the experiences that they actually have. For example, a teacher who sings in the church choir or who has taught herself to play a few guitar chords by ear might feel that such experiences are less relevant than the all-important ability to play the piano. In fact, it could be argued that guitar and vocal skills are far more suited to classroom work, particularly in the early years. When such skills and experiences have been identified, there is a need to decide how they can be put to best effect.

IDENTIFYING DEVELOPMENTAL NEEDS

As well as a skills audit, there are several other ways in which training needs can be identified. For example, in discussions during the planning of the curriculum, it might be found that teachers lack an understanding of what is meant by certain aspects of the programme of study. Monitoring of the delivery of the scheme of work might show that certain elements are not being addressed properly. Gaps might also be identified through internal reviews, inspections by external agencies, self-reviews and staff appraisal.

ESTABLISHING PRIORITIES FOR DEVELOPMENT

Some of the areas in need of development might be common to all staff or might be a particular problem for one or two teachers. Some deficiencies in the staff's knowledge, skills or understanding might be having a more negative impact on pupils' progress than others. By analysing such factors, it should be possible to identify priorities for training.

COSTING THE PROGRAMME

Allied to the prioritising process will be the need to establish costs, in terms of time and money. Decisions will also have to be made on whether the training should be delivered by members of staff within the school or by external providers. Any externally provided course should be carefully researched to ensure that it meets the school's requirements and that it has been well received by other institutions. Where external providers are to deliver training within the school, it is important to furnish them with detailed information to ensure that the precise needs of specific staff are met.

EVALUATION

No matter how carefully an in-service programme is planned, no matter how enjoyable it is and no matter how effective it is in improving teachers' knowledge, it can only be said to be successful if it improves the attainment and progress of pupils. It is against this criterion that any in-service work must ultimately be assessed, although there might be several stages in the evaluation process.

Imagine a school that has run a course on composition. At the end of the first year, the criterion for success might be that everyone makes some attempt to conduct composition activities and to develop some confidence in doing so. In the second year, the success criterion might be that composition is a regular aspect of the planned programme of work delivered by a particular teacher to a class. In the third, the emphasis will be on establishing to what extent the standards of pupils' compositions have improved. Thus the evaluation process becomes gradually more stringent and the focus shifts from the teaching to the impact of that teaching on learning. Unless in-service work is evaluated in these terms, there is no way in which a school can establish whether the investment in training has provided good value for money.

Whether a school organises its own training or draws on external providers, there are several basic principles that need to be borne in mind at the planning and delivery stages and it is to these that we shall now turn our attention.

BASIC PRINCIPLES

The **first principle** is that music should be treated like any other subject. Too often teaching approaches that would be untenable in other subjects have reigned unchallenged in music. For example, the notion of teaching maths as an undifferentiated activity to combined classes of children of mixed ages and abilities would be anathema to most teachers. However, they are prepared to tolerate its musical equivalent – the hymn practice. Most teachers expect that young children should be able to master the principles of language and maths but they are quite happy to accept as authoritative the decision of an 'expert' to exclude a child from the school choir because he or she is 'tone-deaf '. Bad practice is bad practice whatever the subject, and it is foolish to try to make allowances for those practices when they appear in music by claiming that the subject is 'different'.

The **second principle** is that any in-service training activity in music should be to help teachers recognise that, though they may not be trained, experienced, confident musicians, they do have generic teaching skills which are directly applicable to the subject. In this way, they will be encouraged to focus on the positive aspects of their experiences and develop them further.

The **third principle** is that in-service training in music should be based on direct, active experience. The best way to know what something feels like is to feel it and to discover how it tastes is to taste it. The best way to find out about music is to do it. Through this, the teachers will not only develop their personal musicianship but will also be able to appreciate how the children are likely to feel when they are involved in similar activities.

Such experiences will give them insight into issues of how to plan, deliver, monitor and assess teaching and learning in the subject. Therefore, the **fourth principle** is that teachers should draw on their developing experiences to reflect on the nature and purpose of music education.

ACTIVITIES ON WHICH SCHOOL-BASED IN-SERVICE DEVELOPMENT MIGHT BE BASED

In the remainder of this chapter, we shall outline various activities that can be used as a basis for in-service education, in line with the principles identified above. The focus is on in-service that can be organised within the school as part of a series of meetings or workshops. We have assumed that they will be run by the music coordinator but we recognise that many coordinators have had the job thrust upon them and often feel almost as much lack of confidence as their colleagues. To help these teachers, we have provided explanations which some might find too detailed or over prescriptive. However, we make no apology for this. During many years of working with infant teachers and coordinators, it is quite evident that they welcome this approach as a spring-board for developing their own ideas or adapting the suggestions to the specific circumstances in which they are operating.

The activities in the units are by no means exhaustive. They are presented as a guide to what can be done and as a prompt to further thinking and invention. They can be mixed and matched and adapted in the way that staff feel best suits their own needs. This is true both for the sequencing of units and also for the organising of activities within an unit. For example, a unit that progresses from practical activity to listening might be rearranged if it is felt that this will provide a less threatening approach. In each case, however, it is important to give teachers the opportunity to interrelate listening, composing and performing activities and to reflect on their relevance to the work pursued in the classroom. The length of time spent on each unit will depend on the amount of time available for in-service training. As a rough guide, each unit here would take about 1½–2 hours. Whether they should be presented on one or two full days, or over several twilight sessions, is an issue for the school to determine, in the light of its own particular circumstances. We have assumed that the average number of staff involved within an infant school or department will be nine. Depending on the size of staff, the activities will again need to be adapted.

The emphasis in these activities is on helping teachers develop their own level of understanding of basic concepts, musical concepts and terminology, so that they can approach the classroom activities, described elsewhere in the book, with greater confidence.

Unit 1: exploring duration – beat, accent, metre

Purpose

- To enable the teachers to identify and differentiate between beat, accent, metre and rhythm in music, through a combination of listening and performing activities.

Resources

- Recordings of a march (for example, Elgar's *Pomp and Circumstance Marches*); a plainchant (for example, Sequences and Hymns by Hildegard of Bingen); a recitative section from an eighteenth century opera or oratorio (for example, recitatives from Handel's *Messiah* or *Alexander's Feast*) a waltz (for example, 'The Blue Danube Waltz' by Johann Strauss); examples of German or Austrian *Schuhplattler*
- Metronome

Approach

Play the march music to the teachers. When they have listened to it, ask them to move in time to it by marching round the room. Explain that each movement of their feet corresponds to a beat of the music. The beat is the underlying 'pulse' of the music. It can be marked out by marching in this way. It could also be marked in other ways, for example by tapping or clapping or by using visual signs, as in the case of a conductor.

Now play them the plainchant and ask them to move to that. They will find that this time it is impossible to move to the music in a regular way because it does not have a regular underlying pulse or beat. Other examples of music with no regular beat are those short sections of eighteenth century opera or oratorio, called recitatives, where the characters describe what happens in the action. Play the example of a recitative to illustrate this.

Now play the teachers a series of examples which do or do not have beat so that they can get used to the difference. The following are some examples which might be used at this point.

Music with a regular beat

- Handel: *The Arrival of the Queen of Sheba*
- Haydn: Symphony No. 101 in D ('The Clock'), Movement 2, 'Andante'
- Saint-Saens: *Carnival of the Animals*, 'The Elephant'

Music without a regular beat

- Recitatives from Elgar's *The Dream of Gerontius*, Haydn's *Creation*
- Gregorian plainchant
- Fulbert de Chartres: *Chantre de l'an mil*
- Messiaen: *Quatour pour le Fin du Temps*
- Rands: *Wildtrack I*

Next ask the teachers to clap a steady beat in time to a metronome. When they can do this, ask them to count '1, 2, 1, 2' out loud as they clap. Now ask them to clap more loudly each time they say 'one'. They could also stamp their feet on the first beat. Explain that when a beat is made to sound louder than others in this way, it is said to be 'accented'. The occurrence of accents divides the beats into patterns of twos, threes, fours and so on. In a march the accents occur every two beats, therefore the music is said to have a 'metre' of two.

Using the metronome, ask the teachers to clap the beat and to count '1, 2, 3'. Then ask them to accent the first beat in each set of three with a louder clap and/or a stamp. Play them an example of a waltz, explaining that one of the distinguishing features of this type of music is that, in this type of music, the metre is in three.

German and Austrian folk music make considerable use of three-beat metres. It is what gives the distinctive 'oom pah pah' sound to Austrian band music. Folk dancers also often make use of a variety of body sounds to mark the beats. For example, one way of doing so, using claps and thigh slaps is to use a pattern of:

Slap–Clap–Clap

Let the teachers practise this pattern before performing it in time to the extract of Austrian or German folk music.

This activity could be extended by asking the teachers to identify whether a piece of music has two, three or four beats.

Examples of music with 2 beats per bar

- 'Men of Harlech'
- 'The Wearing of the Green'
- 'What Shall We Do With The Drunken Sailor?'

Examples of music with 3 beats per bar

- 'Home on the Range'
- 'Ash Grove'
- 'Amazing Grace'

Examples of music with 4 beats per bar

- 'Any Dream Will Do' from *Joseph and His Amazing Technicolor Dream Coat* by Rice and Lloyd Weber
- 'Swing Low Sweet Chariot'
- 'The Foggy Dew'
- 'Mr Tambourine Man'

Unit 2: exploring tempo

Purpose

- To enable teachers to identify differences and changes in speed (tempo) and to perform, improvise and listen to pieces that differ in tempo or include changes of tempo.

Resources

- Metronome
- Recordings of: Handel's *Largo* and *Flight of the Bumble Bee* by Rimsky-Korsakov.
- Two cards with 'Accelerando' written on one and 'Ritardando' on the other.

Approach

Ask the teachers to clap or move in time to the beat on a metronome. When everyone is doing this accurately, sing a simple, well-known song over the beat for example, 'London's Burning', 'Three Blind Mice', etc.

Now increase the speed of the metronome and repeat the exercise. When this has been done, slow down the metronome and again clap and sing to the beat.

Explain that the term used for speed in music is 'tempo'. In many pieces of music, the precise speed at which the music should move is shown by a 'metronome mark' at the top of the music. It might look like this, for example, ($\downarrow$ = 100) or ($\downarrow$ = 86). Show them examples in actual pieces of music.

In other cases, the music does not have such metronome marks but will use Italian words such as Allegro, Presto, Largo etc. to indicate the speed. Italian terms are used simply because Italian composers were highly influential across Europe at the time when it became common to use words to indicate musical tempo in written scores. In the same way, French terms are used in dancing because of the leading role taken by France at crucial points in the evolution of ballet.

Listen to the recording of Handel's *Largo* and Rimsky-Korsakov's *Flight of the Bumble Bee* and draw attention to the fact that the first is in a slow tempo and the second has a fast tempo. Discuss what other pieces the teachers know which have a slow or a fast tempo.

As well as having a general tempo, pieces can also get faster or slower. The Italian term for getting faster is 'Accelerando'(as in accelerate) and the term for getting slower is 'Ritardando'. In written scores, these are often abbreviated to 'Accel.' or 'Rit.' respectively. Try to find examples of these indications in printed musical scores.

In the next activity, ask the teachers to choose a song which they all know very well. Practise singing it together. When they can do so confidently, take the two cards prepared earlier and explain that, when 'Accelerando' is held up, they should get faster and when 'Ritardando' is shown, they should slow down. Now practise singing the song with variations of tempo. The teachers will soon realise that it is not sufficient to get faster or slower. They will all need to increase or decrease speed at the same rate as each other, otherwise the whole performance will fall apart.

As a follow up to this activity, the teachers could be asked to find pieces which are fast or slow or which get faster or slower as they are performed. These examples will be useful not only to extend their personal understanding but also to supplement the resources available for teaching their pupils.

Unit 3: exploring timbre/tone colour I

Purpose

- To help teachers to understand what is meant by the term 'timbre' and to enable them to identify the use of a variety of individual timbres or combinations of timbres in pieces of music.
- To help make teachers aware of the way that composers have experimented with timbres in order to extend the sound palette available to them.

Resources

- Piano
- Middle C chimebar
- Xylophone
- Tambourine or other unpitched percussion instrument

Recordings of:

- Debussy's *Syrinx*;

- Piece of harpsichord music from the seventeenth or eighteenth centuries for example, a sonata by Scarlatti or a *Prelude and Fugue* by J. S. Bach;
- Solo piano piece by a nineteenth-century composer such as Liszt or Brahms;
- Bartok's Violin Concerto;
- Stockhausen's *Zyklus for Percussion*.

Approach

Ask the teachers to listen to the note Middle C being played on the piano, on a chimebar, on a xylophone. The note is the same pitch each time it is played but its quality changes. This distinctive aspect of the sound is known as its 'timbre' or 'tone colour'. Throughout the centuries, composers have used the tone colour of individual instruments or combinations of instruments to produce a variety of effects.

Play the example of the solo flute from Debussy's *Syrinx* and ask the teachers to find words to describe the sound. They might use words such as 'hollow', 'haunting', 'sad' but will probably find it very difficult. It is easier to recognise the quality of the tone colour of an instrument than to describe it.

Explain that artists not only work with the materials available to them. They are also looking for new materials and new ways of using them to produce particular effects. The colours available to early medieval painters tended to be very dull in comparison with what we have available to use now (Allsopp 1971). Later, painters used egg tempera but this was very fast-drying and meant that artists had to work quickly. The arrival of slow-drying oil paints in the fifteenth century gave artists more freedom to work on their paintings and also enabled them to make their dark colours deeper and more intense. (Richardson 1997). In the nineteenth century, new paints were created, based on chemicals instead of natural pigments. These came in tubes and were easier to pack and made painting out of doors, straight from life, easier (Davidson 1993). It was because of this development that the French Impressionists were able to focus on the changing effects of lights and colours around them. Today artists such as Deirdre Borlase are using computer programs to create their pictures.

In the same way, composers have tried to experiment with methods of extending the range of sounds available to them. At various times, this has involved the creation of new instruments. For example, with the arrival of the piano, composers were able to produce more sustained, louder and varied sounds than had been possible with the earlier harpsichord. To illustrate the differences in sound, play extracts from the selected harpsichord and piano music.

At other times, composers have experimented with finding new sounds in existing instruments by playing them in different ways. The teachers themselves can do this. Ask them to sit in a circle and pass a tambourine around the group. Each teacher should try to find a new way of producing a sound on it. The instrument should keep being passed round until the possibilities have been exhausted. The following are some suggestions of how it might be played: hitting, stroking, scraping, shaking, tapping the wooden part of the instrument, tapping individual jingles, rolling the jingles around, rubbing it with the palm or back of the hand, spinning the tambourine like a plate on the floor and listening to the sounds which it produces as it gets slower and eventually falls over.

The same kind of activity can be pursued with other instruments. For the sake of variety, divide the teachers into groups, with each group exploring the possibilities in a different instrument before sharing the findings with the whole class.

Two twentieth century composers who found a whole range of new timbres by experimenting with percussion were Bartok and Stockhausen. Play extracts from the musical suggestions made above to illustrate some of the effects they created.

Unit 4: exploring timbre/tone colour II

Purpose

• To give teachers further insight into the way that composers have sought to extend the timbre possibilities available to them and to show how this has resulted in the development of electronic music.

Resources

• Stop watch
• Assortment of newspapers and magazines made of different types of paper
• Keyboard

Recordings of:

• John Cage: *Sonatas and Interlude* for prepared piano
• Pierre Schaeffer: *Concert de bruits*
• Pierre Henry: *Le Voile d'Orphée*

Approach

Ask the teachers to sit in a circle. At a sign from you, they should sit in complete and utter silence for 45–60 seconds. You will tell them when the time is up. As they sit there, they will become very conscious of the sounds around them, however soft or distant they might be. When the period of silence is up, ask them to identify, list and discuss the sounds which they heard. Explain that some twentieth century composers have looked to the natural sounds around them for a clue to the extension of the palette of sounds. The American John Cage took this to extremes and produced a piece which consists entirely of 'silence'. Other composers have used the sounds produced by every day objects to extend the range of timbres available to them. This is the equivalent of visual artists using 'found objects' to create sculptures, for example. The term used for this type of music is 'musique concrete' or concrete music and was developed in the late 1940s and early 1950s by a group of French composers, including Pierre Schaeffer and Pierre Henry.

To give the teachers practical experience of this, divide them into groups each with a given task to perform:

• The first group should produce the impression of a windy day, using sounds produced by the hands only.
• The second group should produce a piece which gives the impression of a fire being lit, leaping into life and then dying away. For this they must use the newspapers and magazines. These can be ripped, torn, folded, crumpled etc. to produce a range of sounds.
• The third group should produce an impression of a storm, using wooden and glass surfaces around them.

Each group should first explore the qualities of the sound available to them and then work on deciding which sounds will be most appropriate for the particular task. When they have done this, they should try out and refine their sounds until they are happy with the effect and then prepare a short performance for the rest of the group. When this has been done, listen to a recording of one of the works by Shaeffer suggested in the Resources Section for this unit.

With the increasing availability of tape recorders in the 1950s, composers began to experiment further with such sounds and found that, by recording them and playing them back at faster or slower speeds, the sound palette could be extended even further. Eventually this led to the creation of the electronic synthesiser which enabled composers to decide for themselves precisely how the various waves should behave and, as a result, produced a whole welter of timbres on which they could draw in their compositions.

As a follow up to the above activities, some teachers might like to try to create a sound picture using the more 'unusual' sounds available on the keyboard.

Unit 5: exploring dynamics

Purpose

- To enable teachers to develop their experience and understanding of the concept of dynamics through improvisation and performance activities.

Resources

- An instrument for each teacher
- Large cards, each with one of the following indications written on it: **f, p, ff, pp, mp, mf, <, >,** crescendo (cresc.), decrescendo (decresc.), diminuendo (dim.).

Recordings of:

- the opening of Janáček's *Sinfonietta*;
- the first movement of Beethoven's 'Moonlight' Sonata;
- the opening of Handel's *Zadock the Priest*
- the 'Sabre Dance' from Khachaturian's *Gayane*

Approach

Ask the teachers to sit in a circle, with an instrument each. At a sign from you, they should begin to play their instruments fairly softly. Experiment with bringing the instruments in one after another and then asking the performers to stop one after another. Discuss the effect with them. As the number of instruments increases, the sound gets louder. As the instruments decrease in number, the sound gets softer.

It is also possible to make each instrument loud or soft. Decide on a hand sign which means loud and a sign which means soft. Then ask the instruments to come in one after another. This time, however, some instruments will be played loudly and others softly. Discuss the effects of this and ask the teachers to suggest alternatives and to try these out.

Explain that the use of loud and soft sounds, in various ways and in differing combinations, is an important tool for composers. When referring to differences in volume in pieces, musicians use the term 'dynamics'.

Because of the leading role played by Italians in the development of Western music, we tend to use Italian words to denote loud and soft sounds. The term for loud is **forte** (abbreviated to **f**) and, for **soft**, we use the term **piano** (abbreviated to **p**); hence the term 'pianoforte' for an instrument that can play both soft and loud sounds. There are also gradations represented by the term **mezzo**. Thus **mezzo piano (mp)** = moderately soft and **mezzo forte (mf)** = moderately loud.

Now repeat the earlier exercise. But this time, instead of using hand signs to indicate differences of volume, choose a card for each instrument. Again listen to the effects and discuss and experiment with ways of adapting the music.

Musicians can also produce gradations of volume. The sign < shows that the music gets gradually louder. The term for this in Italian is **crescendo (cresc.)**. The sign for getting gradually softer is > also represented by the **decrescendo (decresc.)** or **diminuendo (dim.)**.

Now repeat the earlier improvisation activity, this time adding these extra signs. From here, the teachers can progress to listening to the suggested recordings and identifying which terms would be most appropriate to describe the relevant sections.

Unit 6: exploring scales I

Purpose

To help teachers understand, through active exploration and listening, that:

- music is often based on specific sets of notes;
- the precise set of notes used influences the nature of the resulting melodies;
- differing sets of notes are associated with music from different times and places.

Resources

Recordings of

- a plainchant melody (for example, by Hildegard von Bingen or Fulbert de Chartres);
- a piece of Chinese music (for example, Fen Yang song from Silver Burdett and Ginn Music Book 3);
- the opening of Debussy's *Prélude à l'après-midi d'un faune*
- 'God Save the Queen'.

Two sets of chromatic chimebars (i.e. sets which include both white and black notes), arranged as follows:

- a) 2 sets of the black notes arranged from the lowest to the highest pitch: C# D# F# G# A#
- b) 1 set of the white chimebars arranged as follows, from the lowest to the highest pitch: C D E F G A B C'
- c) 1 set of white chimebars arranged as follows, from the lowest to the highest pitch:
  D E F G A B C' D'

- d) From the remaining chimebars, arrange 2 sets of notes as follows, from the lowest to the highest pitch:
  C# D# F G A

Approach

Give the teachers a very brief introduction to the pieces before playing each one and asking them to listen very carefully to the music. Discuss the music. Where do they think music comes from? Do all the pieces sound the same? The staff will no doubt recognise the National Anthem and will probably be able to identify the origin of the Chinese music, or at least recognise that it is 'Oriental'. Most will also recognise that the plainchant is associated with 'church music' and dates from several centuries ago. The piece by Debussy might well be more difficult for them to place. Invite them to comment on the music. Then explain that one of the reasons that the pieces sound different is that each piece is based on different sets of notes or 'scales'.

There are as many different types of scales in the world as there are languages and dialects. A scale commonly used in Western Music is the major scale on which the National Anthem is based. This has eight notes and a set pattern of distances between the pitches of the notes contained in it. However, there is no reason why a scale should have eight notes. A great deal of the world's music, for example, is based on five-note scales (pentatonic scales), as in the case of the Chinese folk song heard. Even when a scale has eight notes, they do not have to be arranged in the same way as the notes of a major scale. The plainchant melody and the pieces by Debussy, for example are based on eight note scales but each has its own arrangement of pitch relationships. The plainchant is based on what is known as a mode. Much of traditional and more recent folk music also makes use of modes. The Debussy work, on the other hand makes use of what is termed a 'whole tone scale' because the distance between each of the notes is known as a 'tone'. Other scales make use of a combination of tones and smaller distances or intervals known as 'semi-tones'.

To go beyond this level of detail can become too confusing for some and could detract from the central practical activity described in the next section.

Arrange the chimebars the way described in the Resources section above. Teachers will work individually or in pairs on these sets of notes, depending on the number of staff involved. Ask each individual or pair of teachers to experiment with the sounds and to produce a short melody, using the given notes. Give them about 5 minutes to experiment. Then ask them to begin to decide on a specific format for their tunes, so that they can perform them to the rest of the group. Emphasise that what they are producing is no more than a first draft of their ideas.

After a further five minutes, ask the most confident pair to perform to the rest of the group. Ask them to play their melody twice. Explain that this is to give time for their colleagues to absorb what they are hearing and also to enable them to demonstrate what is intentional and unintentional in their draft composition. Emphasise the need for the performers to ensure that there is a clear moment of silence before their performance starts and also at the end. This 'frame' of silence is necessary to differentiate between the composition and other sounds around. It is the equivalent of the silence in a concert hall after the conductor has entered and before the orchestra starts to play or of the frame around a picture which clearly marks it out from the wall surrounding it.

When the piece has been performed, ask the listeners to comment on what they liked about the melody. This is very different from asking whether they liked it since it leads them into an examination of detail and an exploration of reasons. In other words, it involves the listener in a basic form of appraisal. The next step is to ask the performers to comment on how they might improve their melody. Then invite the rest of the staff to offer suggestions as well. With adults, it can take a little while to get them warmed up with this. This might be because of a reluctance to be seen to 'criticise' the work of colleagues, especially if they are older or enjoy a higher status, or if they are perceived as being 'more musical' than the critic. However, this by no means insurmountable and, with more practice and the realisation that the criticism is constructive, that all will be involved in giving and receiving such comments and that it is not personal but directed at the nature of the composition, even the most reticent adults soon relax and get involved.

After a discussion of how the melody can be redrafted, the composers should have several new ideas on which they can work. The same approach can then be used with the other groups. Alternatively, it might be better to focus on two groups at first and then ask the others to take on board the suggestions made in discussion and to decide whether they can be used to improve their own work.

In this particular activity, the types of suggestions for improvement might focus on the following factors: making the rhythm more interesting; producing an initial idea then a contrasting idea before returning to the original idea; avoiding making the melody too predictable. Many teachers start at the bottom note, progress upwards in pitch from one note to the very next note each time and then come back 'down the scale' in the same way. Encourage them to be more adventurous and to 'leap about' the notes, to give more variety to the sounds. Through a cycle of: experimenting, presenting, discussing, redrafting, further experimenting, each pair should eventually arrive at a finished melody to perform.

Explain that those teachers who are working on the black notes of the chimebars are producing melodies based on pentatonic scales. Those working on the set C D E F G A B C' are working on major scale melodies. Those using the notes D E F G A B C' D' are composing melodies based on a mode. Those working on the remaining set of notes are using a truncated version of whole tone scale.

These tasks have involved the teachers in an integration of listening, improvising, composing, performing and appraising activities. They have also been given information about music which is relevant to the activity and which helps focus their attention and extend their knowledge and understanding. From here, they can develop their interests further. For instance, they could listen to further examples of plainchant or read about scales in reference books.

As a follow up to this activity, teachers could create their own scales and create music based on them. Alternatively, they could use the following African six-note scales:

C D E F G B♭
C E♭ F G A B

Unit 7: exploring texture

Purpose

- To help teachers develop an understanding of what is meant by texture in music
- To introduce them to the concepts of monody, homophony, polyphony and counterpoint

Resources

- Pieces of material, including a piece of tweed and a piece of silk
- Recordings of: a plainchant; J. S. Bach's Toccata and Fugue in D Minor; a section from a piece of traditional jazz; a performance of a traditional hymn sung by a choir of mixed male and female voices.

Approach

Start by asking the teachers to sing a well known round such as 'Three Blind Mice' or 'London's Burning'.

Then ask them to look at the 'weave' of the various pieces of cloth. In the case of the silk, the weave is very tight and it is difficult to see the individual threads. This is very different from the piece of tweed where the individual threads are deliberately designed to be clearly visible. In these circumstances we can say that the texture of each piece of cloth is different.

The term 'texture' has been borrowed by musicians to describe how sounds are blended and how melodies are bound together. Where more than one melody is played or sung the music is said to be making use of **counterpoint**. It has a **contrapuntal** texture. Where the melodies used are more or less the same as each other, the music is said to making use of **imitative counterpoint**. When they sang the round the teachers were performing **imitative counterpoint**.

Play the fugue section from Bach's Toccata and Fugue in D Minor and explain that this is also in imitative counterpoint. If they listen very carefully, they will be able to hear more or less the same idea recurring at various points in the music, just as they can see the same colours in the pattern on a piece of cloth.

Compare this with the recording of the traditional jazz group. Here each instrument is playing its own melody but the melodies tend to be different from each other. The texture of this music is said to represent **non-imitative counterpoint**.

Now ask the teachers to listen to the recording of the traditional hymn. This time there are several voices singing together but there is only one main melody, that is sung by the highest voice. The other voices seem less important and are there simply to 'fill in the harmony'. Music of this type is said to be **homophonic**. Most traditional hymn tunes are of this type.

In the case of some music, there is only one line. Therefore it cannot be said to be either polyphonic or homophonic. Plainchant falls into this category. Play a recording of this type of music and explain that this is known as **monody** or **monodic music**. From here, you could progress to a quiz game where the teachers have to identify what textures are used in a number of new pieces presented to them.

The following pieces are some examples which might be useful for this extension activity:

Imitative counterpoint

- Tallis: *Canon – Glory to Thee My God this Night*
- Pachelbel: *Canon*
- Morley: 'April is in my mistress' face'
- 'Sumer is icumen in'

Non-imitative counterpoint

- Any example of Welsh *penillion* singing
- Vivaldi: 'Autumn' from *The Four Seasons*

Homophony

- Any well known hymn tune

- Mussorgsky: 'The Great Gate of Kiev' (opening section) from *Pictures at an Exhibition*
- Fink: 'I'll Make a Man of You' from *Oh! What a Lovely War*

Monody

- Britten: *Six Metamorphoses After Ovid*

Unit 8: exploring form

Purpose

To give teachers the opportunity to develop their understanding of the concept of form in music through composition, listening and performing activities.

Resources

- A range of pitched and unpitched instruments;
- Recordings of the pieces identified at the end of this unit.

Approach

Divide the teachers into four groups and give each group a combination of pitched and unpitched percussion instruments. The first and second groups should be asked to compose a march each. The third should produce a piece of music which is very fast and very soft. The fourth group should produce a piece which gives the impression of growing and dying away.

Let the teachers experiment with ideas and then present them for comment and redrafting in the way suggested in Unit 6. Eventually they will produce four short pieces. When they have reached this stage, ask Group 1 to join with Group 3 to form a new Group A and for Group 2 to join with Group 4 to form Group B . Each of the new groups should now experiment with ways of combining their original compositions into new shapes or what musicians call 'forms'.

In the case of Group A, for example, a simple shape or form could be created if the music composed by Group 1 were immediately followed by that created by Group 3. The result would be a two-part composition which musicians describe as 'Binary' or 'AB Form'. Another approach is for the first idea to be played, followed by the second and then for the original idea to be played again. A three-part piece of this type is said to be in 'Ternary Form' or 'ABA Form'.

If there is time, the teachers could explore further combinations involving all the groups. For example, they could play a pattern such as the following:

Group 1 Group 2 Group 1 Group 3 Group 1 Group 2 Group 4 Group 1

A piece where the same idea comes round several times in this way is known as a Rondo.

The teachers could then listen to examples of pieces in various forms.

Binary form

- 'Will Ye No Come Back Again?'
- 'Bobby Shaftoe'
- 'Clementine'
- Bach: Minuet in G from the *Anna Magdalena Notebook*

Ternary form

- 'Skye Boat Song'
- Beethoven: Minuet in G
- Bach: Musette from the *Anna Magdalena Notebook*

Rondo form

- Beethoven: Rondo in C, Op. 51, No. 1
- Beethoven: Last movement of Piano Sonata in G, Op. 14, No. 2
- Robert Schumann: 'Intermezzo' from *Carnival Jest*

For the reasons presented earlier, the in-service activities described here focus mainly on developing the teachers' own understanding of the relevant concepts. There is, however, no reason why they could not be related to other sections in this book which focus more specifically on work in the classroom. For example, Unit 1 could be related to the discussion of similar concepts in Chapter 8. Unit 3 could be related to Chapter 7 and so on. By supplementing the units in this way, it will be possible to help teachers increase not only their personal understanding but also their awareness of how the same concepts can be conveyed to young children.

Resources

The following list is by no means exhaustive but should help coordinators in the process of determining what resources would be relevant for their schools.

BOOKS

Information books for teachers

British Music Education Yearbook
Rheingold Publishing Ltd,
241 Shaftesbury Avenue, London WC2H 8EH

Come on Everybody, Let's Sing
Lois Birkenshaw Fleming
Gordon V. Thompson, Canada.
(Available in UK from Lovely Music)

Gently into Music
Mary York
Longman

Introducing Music at Key Stage 1
C. Kempton
Southgate

Making Sense of Music
Colin Durrant and Graham Welch
Cassell Education

Music Education In Theory and Practice
Charles Plummeridge
The Falmer Press

Music for Fun, Music for Learning
Lois Birkenshaw
Holt, Rheinhart and Winston

Music in the Primary School revised edition
Janet Mills
Cambridge University Press

Take Note
Leonora Davies
BBC Educational Publishing

Teaching Music in the National Curriculum
George Pratt and John Stephens
Heinemann

The Sounding Symbol
George Odam
Stanley Thornes (Publishers) Ltd.

What Primary Teachers Should Know About Music
d'Reen Struthers
Hodder and Stoughton

Information books for children

'Famous Children Series':
Bach
Brahms
Chopin
Handel
Haydn
Mozart
Schumann
Tchaikovsky
Gollancz Children's Paperbacks

Listen
Ginn Science
Level 2

Music
Illustrated by Donald Grant
Created by Gallimard Jeunesse and Claude Delafosse
Moonlight Publishing/First Discovery

The Orchestra
Mark Rubin and Alan Daniel
Oxford University Press

MUSIC COURSES FOR THE EARLY YEARS

Blueprints: Music Key Stage 1
Aelwyn Pugh
(Teacher's resource book, photocopiable materials and cassette)
Stanley Thornes

Bright Ideas: Music
Richard Addison
Scholastic

Carousel Primary Music
Joan Child, Richard Crozier and Ken Storry
(Teacher's books, Cassettes / CDs, Group Discussion Books – fully photo-copiable)
Ginn and Company

Growing with Music (Somerset Music Education Programme)
Stage 1
Michael Stocks and Andrew Maddocks
(Book, cassette and photocopiable material)
Longman

High Low Dolly Pepper
Veronica Clark
A & C Black

Let's Make Music: Music for All
Prill and Martin Hinkley
Topics for Key Stage 1
(Book and cassette)
Novello / Music Sales

Music All the Time
Wendy Bird and Elizabeth Bennett
(Teacher's book, pupils' book and cassette)
Chester / Music Sales

Music Connections
Kate Buchanan and Stephen Chadwick
(Teacher's book and CDs)
Cramer Music

Music Starting Points with Young Children
Jean Gilbert
Ward Lock Educational

Music Through Topics
Veronica Clark
(Book and cassette)
Cambridge University Press

Music With Mr Plinkerton
Eleanor Gamper
Ward Lock Educational and IMP

Musical Growth in the Elementary School
B. Bergethon, E. B. Meske and J. Montgomery
Holt, Rinehart and Winston

Nelson Music 1
Mary Edwards and Lis Fletcher
(Book and cassettes/CDs)
Thomas Nelson

Oxford Primary Music
Leonora Davies and Jean Gilbert
Key Stage 1
(Teacher's book, pupils' books and cassette)
Oxford University Press

Recipe Book 1, 2 and 3
Jan Holstock
Lovely Music

Silver Burdett Music
Book 1
English Edition edited by George Odam
(Teacher's book, charts and cassettes)
Stanley Thornes

Sounds of Music
Books 1 and 2
G. Odam, J. Arnold and A. Ley
(Teacher's book, posters and CDs)
Stanley Thornes

Sounds Topical
Jan Holstock
Oxford University Press

Targeting Music
Book 1: Reception
Book 2: Year 1
Book 3: Year 2
Dorothy Taylor
Schott

Vocal music

Big Book of Children's Songs
Eileen Diamond
(Book and Cassette)
IMP

Birds and Beasts
Edited by Sheena Roberts
A & C Black

Bobby Shaftoe Clap Your Hands
Sue Nicholls
A & C Black

Easy Mix 'n' Match
David Jenkins and Mark Visocchi
Universal Edition

Eileen Diamond Super Songbooks
Book 1
(Book and Cassette)
Universal Edition

Hubble Bubble
Alison Hedger
(Book and Cassette)
Music Sales (Golden Apple)

Kokoleoko
June Tillman
Macmillan

Light the Candles
June Tillman
Cambridge University Press

Look Lively, Rest Easy
Edited by Helen East
(Book and cassette)
A & C Black

Mango Spice: 44 Caribbean Songs
Yvonne Conolly, Gloria Cameron and Sonia Singham Vallin Miller
A & C Black

Oranges and Lemons
Karen King
Illustrated by Ian Beck
(Book and cassette)
Oxford University Press

Our Street
Jan Holstock
Lovely Music

Pompaleerie Jig
D. Thompson and K. Baxter
Arnold Wheaton

Sing a Song
Wendy Bird, David Evans and Gary McAuliffe
(Book and Video)
Thomas Nelson & Sons Ltd

Sonsense Nongs
Michael Rosen
A & C Black

The Music Box Songbook
Barry Gibson
BBC

Trig Trog
Douglas Coombes
Oxford University Press

Turnip Head
Jan Holstock
Lovely Music

Zmm Zmm
Douglas Coombes
Oxford University Press

Vocal and instrumental music

Catch a Round
Peter Sidaway
Beaters Series
Schott

Jason Jones
David Moses
Beaters Series
Schott

Adventures in Music for the Very Young Child
Gillian Wakeley
Beaters Series
Schott

Recorder tutors

Abracadabra Recorder
Book 1
A & C Black

Me and My Recorder
Part 1
Marlene Hobsbawm
Faber Music

Playtime
Margot Fagan
(Teacher's book)

Play Together
(Ensemble book)
Longman

Special needs resources

Earwiggo 1, 2 and 3
Jan Holstock and Mavis West
Lovely Music

Gently into Music
M. York
Longman

Making Music Special
John Childs
David Fulton Publishers

Music for All
Peter Wills and Melanie Peter
David Fulton Publishers

Pied Piper
John Bean and Amelia Oldfield
Cambridge University Press

The Music Curriculum and Special Educational Needs
National Association of Special Educational Needs

Up, Up and Away
Derek Pearson
Oxford University Press

Wonderful Me
Caroline Hoile
Music Sales/Golden Apple
(Book and cassette)

Resources for topic and cross curricular work

Carousel Primary Music
Joan Child, Richard Crozier and Ken Storry
(Teacher's books, Cassettes/CDs, Group Discussion Books – fully photo-
copiable)
Ginn and Company

Explore Music Series:
Explore Music through Art
Explore Music through Geography
Explore Music through History
Explore Music through Maths
Explore Music through Movement
Explore Music through Poetry and Rhyme
Explore Music through Science
Explore Music through Stories
Explore Music through Word Games
David Wheway and Shelagh Thomson
Oxford University Press

Festivals
Jean Gilbert
(Teacher's book and cassette)
Oxford University Press

Junkanoo
S. Winfield and D. Thompson
Universal

Let's Make Music: Music for All
Prill and Martin Hinkley
Topics for Key Stage 1
(Book and cassette)
Novello/Music Sales

Music Through Topics
Veronica Clark
(Book and cassette)
Cambridge University Press

Sound Ideas
Patricia Binns and Marle Chacksfield
Oxford University Press

Sounds of Music
Books 1 and 2
G. Odam, J. Arnold and A. Ley
(Teacher's book, posters and CDs)
Stanley Thornes

Sounds Topical
Jan Holstock
Oxford University Press

Story, Song and Dance
Jean Gilbert
Cambridge University Press

Three Singing Pigs
Kaye Umansky
A & C Black

Whoopsey Diddley Dandy Dee
S. Whitfield and D. Thompson
Universal

USEFUL MAGAZINES AND JOURNALS

BBC Music Magazine
Primary Music
Music Teacher Magazine
British Journal of Music Education

PROFESSIONAL ASSOCIATION

National Association of Music Educators,
56 Hall Orchard Lane,
Frisby-on-the-Wreake,
Melton Mowbray,
Leicestershire
LE14 2NH

INSTRUMENTS AND EQUIPMENT

We suggest that ideally each class in the infant school should contain the following equipment:

Untuned/unpitched percussion

afuche	drums	tambourines
cabasa	guiro	castanets
bells	claves	maracas
cymbals	rattles	finger cymbals
shakers	Indian bells	tambour

Tuned (pitched) percussion

agogos	cow bells	chimebars
glockenspiels	xylophones	metallophones

Other tuned instruments

Instruments for blowing: recorders, melodicas, whistles etc.
guitar
keyboard

Audio equipment

Tape recorder and/or listening centre

Recordings

Cassettes & CDs of music from a wide range of cultural and historical origins.

Each class should also have access to computer software, details of which have been provided in Chapter 10.

Bibliography

Abeles, H. and Porter, S. (1978) Sex-stereotyping of musical instruments. *Journal of Research in Music Education*, 26 (2), 65–75.

Addison, R. (1987) *Bright Ideas – Music*. Leamington Spa: Scholastic Publications.

Allen, S. (1988) Case studies of music consultancy. *British Journal of Music Education*, 6, 2, 139.

Allsopp, B. (1971) *Romanesque Architecture*. London: Arthur Barker Ltd.

Aspin, D. (1984) *Objectivity and Assessment in the Arts: The Problem of Aesthetic Education*. National Association for Education in the Arts.

Baker, R. (1975) *The Magic of Music*. New York: Universe Books.

Barrett, M. (1994) Music education and the primary/early childhood teacher: a solution. *The British Journal of Music Education*, 11 (3), 197–207.

Beard, R. M. (1969) *An Outline of Piaget's Developmental Psychology*. London: Routledge and Kegan Paul.

Ben-Tovim, A. (1979) *Children and Music*. London: A & C Black.

Bentley, A. (1965) *Musical Ability in Children and its Measurement*. London: Harrap and Co. Ltd.

Bentley, A. (1975) *Music in Education: A Point of View*. Windsor: NFER Publishing Company.

Bergethon, B., Meske, E. B., and Montgomery, J. (1986) *Musical Growth in the Elementary School* (Fifth Edition). New York: Holt, Rinehart and Winston.

Berry, M. (1976) Justine Ward in Simpson, K. (ed.) *Some Great Music Educators*. London: Novello and Co.

Bird, W. and Bennett, E. (1988) *Music All The Time*. London: Chester/Music Sales.

Bloom, B. F. (1956 and 1964) *Taxonomy of Educational Objectives: A Classification of Educational Goals*. 2 vols. London: Longburn.

Board of Education (1937) *Handbook of Suggestions*. London: HMSO.

Bowers, J. and Tick, J. (1986) *Women Making Music*. London: Macmillan.

Brocklehurst, B. (1971) *Response to Music*. London: Routledge and Kegan Paul.

Bryant, P. and Bradley, L. (1985) *Children's Reading Problems*. Oxford: Blackwell.

Busoni, F. (1911) (Trans. Baker, T.) Sketch of a new aesthetic of music. New York: Schirmer; reprinted (1962) in *Three Classics in the Aesthetics of Music*. New York: Dover.

Calouste Gulbenkian Foundation (1982) *The Arts in Schools: Principles, Practice and Provision*. Calouste Gulbenkian Foundation.

Cambridgeshire Report (1933) *Music and the Community*. London: Cambridge University Press.

Carlton, N. (1987) *Music in Education: A Guide for Parents and Teachers*. London: The Woburn Press.

Chapius, J. (1979) (Trans. Miller, R.) *Initiating Children to Music*. Fribourg: Editions 'Pro Musica'.

Choksy, L. (1974) *The Kodály Method*. New Jersey: Prentice-Hall Inc.

Cleall, C. (1968) The natural pitch of the human voice. Paper presented at BPS Annual Conference (Education Section), Didsbury, September 1968.

Cole, H. (1974) *Sounds and Signs, Aspects of Musical Notation*. London: Oxford University Press.

Cooke, D. (1959) *The Language of Music*. London: Oxford University Press.

Copland, A. (1952) *Music and Imagination*. New York: The New American Library.

Curwen, J. (1858) *Standard Course of Tonic Sol-Fa*. London: Curwen.

Davidson, L. *et al.* (1981) cited in Davies, C. (1992) Listen to my song: a study of songs invented by children aged 5 to 7 years. *British Journal of Music Education*, 9 (1), 19–48.

Davidson, R. (1993) *What is Art?* Oxford: Oxford University Press.

Davies, C. (1986) Say it till a song comes (reflections on songs invented by children 3–13). *British Journal of Music Education*, 3 (3), 279–93.

Davies, C. (1992) Listen to my song: a study of songs invented by children aged 5 to 7 years. *British Journal of Music Education*, 9 (1), 19–48.

Davies, I. (1971) Music, in Whitfield, R. C. (ed.) *Disciplines of the Curriculum*, 186–199. London: McGraw-Hill.

Dearden, R. F. (1976) *Problems in Primary Education*. London: Routledge and Kegan Paul.

Department of Education and Science (1967) *Children and their Primary Schools. A Report of the Central Advisory Council for Education (England)*, ('Plowden Report') London: HMSO.

Department of Education and Science (1978) *Primary Education in England: A Survey by HM Inspectors of Schools*. London: HMSO.

Department of Education and Science (1981) *Aesthetic Development: A Report for the Assessment of Performance Unit, Exploratory Group on Aesthetic Development*. London: HMSO.

Department of Education and Science (1982) *Education 5 to 9: An Illustrative Survey of 80 First Schools in England*. London: HMSO.

Department of Education and Science (1985) *Curriculum Matters 4: Music from 5 to 16*. London: HMSO.

Department of Education and Science (1987) *The National Curriculum Task Group on Assessment and Testing – A Report*. London: HMSO.

Department of Education and Science (1988) *Better Schools*. London: HMSO.

Department of Education and Science (1989) *Planning for School Development: Advice to Governor, Headteachers and Teachers. School development plans project 1*. London: HMSO.

Department of Education and Science (1991a) *National Curriculum Music Working Group Interim Report*. London: HMSO.

Department of Education and Science (1991b) *The Implementation of the Curricular Requirements of ERA: An Overview of HM Inspectorate on the First Year, 1989–90*. London: HMSO.

Deutsch, D. (ed.) (1982) *The Psychology of Music*, 413–429. New York: Academic Press.

Dewey, J. (1958) *Arts as Experience*. New York: Capricorn Books.

Dowling, J. (1982) Melodic information processing and its development, in Deutsch, D. (ed.) *The Psychology of Music*. New York: Academic Press.

Dowling, J. (1984) Development of musical schemata in children's spontaneous singing in Crozier, W. R. and Chapman, A. J. (eds) *Cognitive Processes in the Perception of Art*, 145–163. Amsterdam: Elsevier.

Durrant, C. and Welch, G. (1995) *Making Sense of Music*. London: Cassell Education.
Fletcher, P. (1987) *Education and Music*. Oxford and New York: Oxford University Press.
Gamper, E. (1986) *Music With Mr Plinkerton*. London: Ward Lock Educational.
Gardner, H. (1983) *Frames of Mind: The Theory of Multiple Intelligences*. London: Heinemann.
Gifford, E. (1993) The musical training of primary teachers: old problems, new insights and possible solutions. *British Journal of Music Education*, 10 (1), 33.
Gilbert, J. (1981) *Musical Starting Points with Young Children*. London: Ward Lock Educational.
Gwynn Williams, W. S. (1971) *Welsh National Music and Dance* (Fourth Edition). Llangollen: The Gwynn Publishing Company.
Hadow, W. H. (Chairman) (1926) *Report of the Consultative Committee of the Board of Education on The Education of the Adolescent*. London: HMSO.
Hancox, G. (1982) Music education and industry, in Paynter, J. *Music in the Secondary School Curriculum*. Schools Council, Cambridge: Cambridge University Press.
Hargreaves, D. J. (1986) *The Developmental Psychology of Music*. Cambridge: Cambridge University Press.
Hennessy, S. (1995) *Music 7–11: Developing Primary Teaching Skills*. London and New York: Routledge.
Hermann, E. J. (1965) *Supervising Music in the Elementary School*. Englewood Cliffs, New Jersey: Prentice-Hall.
Hindemith, P. (1952) *A Composer's World*. Gloucester, Mass.: Harvard University Press.
Hirst, P. H. (1974) *Knowledge and the Curriculum*. London: Routledge.
Hirst, P. H. and Peters, R. S. (1970) *Logic of Education*. London: Routledge and Kegan Paul, Students Library of Education.
Howe, M. J. A. and Sloboda, J. (1991a) Young musicians' accounts of significant influences in their early lives: 1 The family and musical background. *British Journal of Music Education*, 8 (1), 39.
Howe, M. J. A. and Sloboda, J. (1991b) Young musicians' accounts of significant influences in their early lives: 2 Teachers, practising and performing. *British Journal of Music Education*, 8 (1), 53.
James, J. (1993) *The Music of the Spheres*. London: Abacus.
Kalmar, M. (1982) The effects of music education based on Kodály's directives in nursery school children – from a psychologist's point of view. *Psychology of Music*, special issue, 63–67.
Keetman, G. (1970) *Elementaria: First Acquaintance with Orff-Schulwerk*. (English translation by Murray, M., 1974) London: Schott and Co. Ltd.
Keetman, G. (1974) *Elementaria*. (English translation by Murray, M., 1974) London: Schott and Co. Ltd.
Kemp, A. (1990) Kinaesthesia in music and its implications for development in microtechnology. *British Journal of Music Education*, 7 (3), 223.
Kempton, C. (1991) *Introducing Music at Key Stage 1*. Crediton: Southgate.
Lamp, C. J. and Keys, N. (1935) Can aptitude for specific musical instruments be predicted? *American Journal of Educational Psychology*, 26, 587–96.
Land, L. R. and Vaughan, M. A. (1978) *Music in Today's Classroom: Creating, Listening, Performing* (Second Edition). San Diego: Harcourt Brace Jovanovich Inc.
Langer, S. K. (1957) *Problems of Art*. New York: Charles Scribner's Sons.
Lawton, D. (1973) *Social Change, Educational Theory and Curriculum Planning*. London: Hodder and Stoughton.

Mark, M. L. (1978) *Contemporary Music Education*. New York: Schirmer Books.

Mark, M. L. (1982) *The Evolution of Music Education Philosophy from Utilitarian to Aesthetic*, cited in Temmerman, N. (1991) The philosophical foundations of music education: the case for primary music education in Australia. *British Journal of Music Education*, 8 (2), 149.

McKernon, P. (1979) The development of first songs in young children in Gardner, H. and Wolf, D. (eds) *Early Symbolisation*. San Francisco: Jossey Bass.

Mead, M. (1964) Comments in Sebeaok, T. A., Hayes, A. S. and Bateson, M. C. (eds) *Approaches to Semiotics*. The Hague: Mouton.

Meyer-Denkmann, G. (1977) *Experiments in Sound*. London: Universal Edition.

Mills, J. (1989) The generalist primary teacher of music: a problem of confidence. *British Journal of Music Education*, 6 (2), 125–38.

Mills, J. (1991) *Music in the Primary School*. Cambridge: Cambridge University Press.

Ministry of Education (1967) *Children and their Primary Schools* ('Plowden Report'). London: HMSO.

Montessori, M. (1936) *The Secret of Childhood*. Calcutta: Orient Longmans.

Moog, H. (English Edition, 1976) *The Musical Experience of the Pre-school Child*. London: Schott and Co. Ltd..

Moses, D. (1984) *Jason Jones: An Instant Music Programme for Younger Primary Children*. London: Schutt.

Moutrie, J. (1976) The Appreciation Movement in Britain: Macpherson, Read and Scholes in Simpson, K. (ed.) *Some Great Music Educators*, 60–68. London: Novello and Co.

Muir, F. (1976) *The Frank Muir Book: An Irreverent Companion to Social History*. London: Heinemann.

Music Education Council (1997) *Music Education Manifesto for the Millennium*. London: MEC.

Naumann, E. (n.d.) *The History of Music*. London: Cassell (trans. F. Pragler), cited in Durrant and Welch (1995) *Making Sense of Music*. London: Cassell Education.

Neuls-Bates, C. (1982) *Women in Music*. New York: Harper and Row.

Nketia, J. H. K. (1986) *The Music of Africa*. London: Victor Gollancz Ltd.

Odam, G. (1995) *The Sounding Symbol: Music Education in Action*. Cheltenham; Stanley Thornes (Publishers) Ltd.

Odam, G. (ed.) (1989) *Silver Burdett Music*. Simon and Schuster.

OFSTED (1994) *Improving Schools*. London: HMSO.

OFSTED (1995a) *Guidance on the Inspection of Nursery and Primary Schools*. London: HMSO.

OFSTED (1995b) *Music: A Review of Inspection Findings 1993/94*. London: HMSO.

OFSTED (1996) *A Review of Inspection Findings 1993/1994*. London: HMSO.

Okafor, R. (1989) Of ditties, need and amnesia – music and primary education in Anambra State, Nigeria. *British Journal of Music Education*, 6 (2), 3.

Ostwald, P. (1973) *Musical Behaviour in Early Childhood*, cited in Schuter-Dyson, R. and Gabriel, C. (1981) *The Psychology of Musical Ability* (Second Edition). London: Methuen.

Paynter, J. (1982) *Music in the Secondary School Curriculum*. Schools Council, Cambridge: Cambridge University Press.

Peter, L. J. (1991) *5,000 Gems of Wit and Wisdom*. London: Treasure Press.

Phenix, P. H. (1964) *The Realms of Meaning*. London: McGraw-Hill.

Plummeridge, C. (1991) *Music Education in Theory and Practice*. London: The Falmer Press.

Pointon, M. (1980) Mucking about with noises: a reply to Aelwyn Pugh, *Cambridge Journal of Education*, 10, 1, 35–9.

Pratt, G. and Stephens, J (eds) (1995) *Teaching Music in the National Curriculum*. Oxford: Heinemann Educational Publishers.

Pugh, A. (1979) Attitudes to music: a study of variables. Unpublished M.Ed. Dissertation, University College of Wales, Aberystwyth.

Pugh, A. (1980) In defence of musical literacy, *Cambridge Journal of Education*, 10, 1, 19–34.

Pugh, A. (1991) *Women in Music*. Cambridge: Cambridge University Press.

Pugh, A. (1994) *Blueprints: Music Key Stage 1*. Cheltenham: Stanley Thornes (Publishers) Ltd.

Pugh, A. and Pugh, L. (1995) *Blueprints: Music Key Stage 2*. Cheltenham: Stanley Thornes (Publishers) Ltd.

Rainbow, B. (ed.) (1968) *Handbook for Music Teachers*. London: Novello and Co.

Read, G. (1964) *Music Notation: A Manual of Modern Practice*. Boston: Allyn and Bacon Inc.

Reid, A. (1979) Foreword to Swanwick, K. *A Basis for Music Education*. Windsor: NFER Publishing Company.

Reimer, B.(1970) *A Philosophy of Music Education*. New Jersey: Prentice Hall.

Richardson, J. (1997) *Looking at Pictures*. London: A & C Black.

Ross, M. (1975) *Art and the Adolescent: Schools Council Working Paper 54*. London: Evans/Methuen Educational.

Russell-Smith, G. (1977a) *Be a Real Musician*. London: Boosey and Hawkes.

Russell-Smith, G. (1977b) *Be a Better Musician*. London: Boosey and Hawkes.

Sachs, C. (1943) *The Rise of Music in the Ancient World: East and West*. New York: Norton.

Salaman, W. (1983) *Living School Music*. Cambridge: Cambridge University Press.

Scholes, P. A. (ed. Ward, J. O.) (1972) *The Oxford Companion to Music* (Tenth Edition). London: Oxford University Press.

Schools Curriculum and Assessment Authority (1995) *Consistency in Teacher Assessment*. London: SCAA Publications.

Schools Curriculum and Assessment Authority (1997) *Criteria and Procedures for the Accreditation of Baseline Assessment Schemes*, Revised Draft. London: SCAA.

Schuter-Dyson, R. and Gabriel, C. (1981) *The Psychology of Musical Ability* (Second Edition). London: Methuen.

Schweitzer, A. (1905) *Bach*. Paris 1905, Leipzig 1908; English translation by E. Newman, London: 1911; revised edition: 1952.

Scrimshaw, P. (1974) Statements, language and art: some comments on Professor Hirst's paper. *Cambridge Journal of Education*, 3, 3, 44.

Serafine, M. L. (1988) *Music as Cognition*. New York: Columbia University Press.

Shiobara, M. (1994) Music and movement: the effect of movement on musical comprehension. *British Journal of Music Education*, 11 (1), 113.

Sidaway, P. (1984) *Strike Five*. London: Schott.

Simpson K. (ed.) (1976) *Some Great Music Educators*. London: Novello and Co.

Sloboda, J. (1985) *The Musical Mind*. Oxford: Clarendon Press.

Stravinsky, I. (1947) *Poetics of Music*. New York: Vintage Books.

Swanwick, K. (1979) *A Basis for Music Education*. Windsor: NFER Publishing Company.

Swanwick, K. (1988) *Music, Mind and Education*. London: Routledge.

Swanwick, K. (1994) *Musical Knowledge: Intuition, Analysis and Music Education*. London and New York: Routledge.

Swanwick, K. and Tillman, J. (1986) The sequence of musical development: a study of children's composition. *British Journal of Music Education*, 3 (3), 305.

Taylor, D. (1979) *Music Now*. Milton Keynes: The Open University.

Taylor, D. (1989) Physical movement and memory for music. *British Journal of Music Education*, 6 (3), 251.

Taylor, M. (1986) Music profiles – a pilot scheme. *British Journal of Music Education*, 3 (1), 19.

Teacher Training Agency (1995) *School-Centred Initial Teacher Training*. London: HMSO.

Teacher Training Agency (1996) *Effective Training Through Partnership*. London: HMSO.

Teacher Training Agency (1997) *Training Curriculum and Standards for New Teachers – proposed new initial teacher training course requirements*. London: TTA.

Temmerman, N. (1991) The philosophical foundations of music education: the case for primary music education in Australia. *British Journal of Music Education*, 8 (2), 149.

Terry, P. (1994) Musical notation in secondary education: some aspects of theory and practice. *British Journal of Music Education*, 11 (1) 99.

Tolstoy, L. (1898) *What Is Art?* (trans. Aylmer Maude). London: OUP, 1969.

University of Westminster (1996) *The Value of Music*. London: National Music Council.

Vulliamy, G. and Lee, E. (1980) *Pop, Rock and Ethnic Music in School*. Cambridge: Cambridge University Press.

Vulliamy, G. and Shepherd, J. (1984a) The application of a critical sociology to music education. *British Journal of Music education*, 1 (3), 247.

Vulliamy, G. and Shepherd, J. (1984b) Sociology and music education; a reply to Swanwick. *British Journal of Music Education*, 5 (1), 57.

Wakeley, G. (1984) *Adventures in Music for the Very Young*. London: Schott.

The Walker Bear Children's Treasury. London: Walker Books.

Weiss, P. and Taruskin, R. (1984) cited in Temmerman (1991).

Welch, G. F. (1985a) Viability of practice and knowledge of results as factors in learning to sing in tune. Paper to the 10th ISME Research Seminar, June 29–July 5, 1984. University of Victoria, B.C., Canada, in *Bulletin of the Council for Research in Music Education*, 85, 238–247.

Welch, G. F. (1985b) A scheme theory of how children learn to sing in tune. *Psychology of Music*, 13, 3–18.

Welch, G. F. (1986) A developmental view of children's singing. *British Journal of Music Education*, 3 (3), 295.

Whitfield, R. C. (ed.) (1971) *Disciplines of the Curriculum*. London: McGraw-Hill.

Wisbey, A. (1980) *Music as the Source of Learning*. Lancaster: MTP.

Wishart, T. (1977) Musical writing, musical speaking, in Shepherd, Virden, Vullimay and Wishart, *Whose Music? A Sociology of Musical Languages*. London: Latimer New Dimensions.

Witkin, R. W. (1974) *The Intelligence of Feeling*. London: Heinemann Educational Books.

Wragg, E. C., Bennett, S. N. and Carre, C. G. (1989) Primary teachers and the National Curriculum, *Research Papers in Education*. Windsor: NFER Nelson Publishing Company.

Index